Corporations and Partnerships in Sweden

Corporations and Partnerships in Sweden

Second Edition

Magdalena Giertz
Carl Hemström (†)

This book was originally published as a monograph in the International Encyclopaedia of Laws/Corporations and Partnerships.

General Editors: Roger Blanpain, Frank Hendrickx
Volume Editor: Koen Geens

Wolters Kluwer
Law & Business

Published by:
Kluwer Law International
PO Box 316
2400 AH Alphen aan den Rijn
The Netherlands
Website: www.kluwerlaw.com

Sold and distributed in North, Central and South America by:
Aspen Publishers, Inc.
7201 McKinney Circle
Frederick, MD 21704
United States of America
Email: customer.service@aspenpublishers.com

Sold and distributed in all other countries by:
Turpin Distribution Services Ltd.
Stratton Business Park
Pegasus Drive, Biggleswade
Bedfordshire SG18 8TQ
United Kingdom
Email: kluwerlaw@turpin-distribution.com

ISBN 978-90-411-6159-8

This title is available on www.kluwerlawonline.com

The Authors

Professor Emeritus Carl Hemström was professor of private law at the universities of Stockholm and Uppsala. He wrote widely on the law of companies, partnerships, economic (cooperative) societies, non-profit associations and foundations.

Since the death of Prof. Carl Hemström in March 2011, Magdalena Giertz has been taking over the updating of all Hemström's previous works. Magdalena Giertz (MML) has previous worked at the Department of Business Law at Uppsala university, and is now attached to the Law Faculty at the same university.

The second edition of this monograph has been reviewed by Magdalena Giertz.

The Authors

Table of Contents

Preface

This book gives an account of Swedish law in the area of companies and partnerships. While working on the first edition of this text, Carl Hemström made use of the Swedish Companies Act 2005 as translated by Reuven Ben-Dor MA (Cantab), TransLegal Sweden AB, and published by Norstedts Juridik – always, however, giving due consideration to the Swedish original – and there has been no reason to make any changes regarding this matter while working on the second edition.

LLD Mikael Hansson (Senior Lecturer of the Law Department, Uppsala University) has been kind enough to read and comment on the pages of labour law.

Any comments on this book can be sent to Magdalena Giertz, Juridicum, Box 512, 751 20 Uppsala, Sweden or emailed to Magdalena.Giertz@jur.uu.se.

List of Abbreviations

CSD	Central Securities Depository
EC	European Council
EEA	European Economic Area
EEC	European Economic Community
EU	European Union
MiFID	Markets in Financial Instruments Directive
SE	Societas Europea
SEK	Swedish Krona

List of Abbreviations

List of Cited Acts, Official Bodies, Etc.

Accounting Act 1999 *(bokföringslag 1999:1078)*.
Annual Reports Act 1995 (*årsredovisningslag* 1995:1554).
Arbitration Act 1999 (*lag* 1999:116 *om skiljeförfarande*).
Board Representation for Employees in the Private Sector, Act on, 1987 (*lag* 1987:1245 *om styrelserepresentation för de privatanställda*).
Business Names Act 1974 (*firmalag* 1974:156).
Codetermination in Working Life, Act on, 1976 (*lag* 1976:580 *om medbestämmande i arbetslivet*).
Companies Act 2005 (*aktiebolagslag* 2005:551).
Companies Registration Office (*Bolagsverket*).
County Administrative Board (*Länsstyrelsen*).
Debt Recovery Code (*utsökningsbalk*).
Educational Leave Act 1974 (*lag* 1974:981 *om arbetstagares rätt till ledighet för utbildning*).
Financial Advices for Consumers Act 2003 (*lag* 2003:862 *om finansiell rådgivning till konsumenter*).
Financial Instruments (Accounts) Act 1998 (*lag* 1998:1479 *om kontoföring av finansiella instrument*).
Financial Instruments Trading Act 1991 (*lag* 1991:980 *om handel med finansiella instrument*).
Financial Supervisory Authority (*Finansinspektionen*).
Identification Designations for Artificial Persons etc., Act on, 1974 (*lag* 1974:174 *om identitetsbeteckning för juridiska personer m.fl.*).
Institute for Accounting Profession in Sweden (*FAR*).
Joint Ownership Act 1904 (*lag* 1904:48 *s.1 om samäganderätt*).
Litigation in Labour Disputes, Act on, 1974 (*lag* 1974:371 *om rättegången i arbetstvister*).
Market Misuse, Act on Penalty for, 2005 (*lag* 2005:377 *om straff för marknadsmissbruk vid handel med finansiella instrument*).
National Insurance Act 1962 (*lag* 1962:381 *om allmän försäkring*).
Notification Obligation Act on Holding of Financial Instruments 2000 (*lag* 2000:1087 *om anmälningsskyldighet för vissa innehav av finansiella instrument*).
Official Gazette (*Post-och Inrikes Tidningar*).
Parental Code (*föräldrabalk*).
Partnerships Act 1980 (*lag* 1980:1102 *om handelsbolag och enkla bolag*).
Penal Code (*brottsbalk*).

List of Cited Acts, Official Bodies, Etc.

Pension Commitments (Security) Act 1967 (*lag* 1967:531 *om tryggande av pensionsutfästelse m.m.*).
Position of Trade Union Representatives at the Workplace Act 1974 (*lag* 1974:358 *om facklig förtroendemans ställning på arbetsplatsen*).
Promissory Notes Act 1936 (*lag* 1936:81 *om skuldebrev*).
Public Takeover Bids on the Stock Market Act 2006 (*lag* 2006:451 *om offentliga uppköpserbjudanden på aktiemarknaden*).
Qualified Electronic Signatures Act 2000 (*lag* 2000:832 *om kvalificerade elektroniska signaturer*).
Regulations of the Financial Supervisory Authority (*Finansinspektionens författningssamling*).
Securities Market Act 2007 (*lag* 2007:528 *om värdepappersmarknaden*).
Security of Employment Act 1982 (*lag* 1982:80 *om anställningsskydd*).
State Borrowing and Debt Management Act 1988 (*lag* 1988:1387 *om statens upplåning och skuldförvaltning*).
Supervisory Board of Public Accountants (*Revisorsnämnden*).
Swedish Industry and Commerce Stock Exchange Committee (*Näringslivets Börskommitte, NBK*).
Swedish Securities Committee (*Aktiemarknadsnämnden*).
Trade Registers Act 1974 (*handelsregisterlag* 1974:157).
Vacations Act 1977 (*semesterlag* 1977:480).
Working Environment Act 1977 (*arbetsmiljölag* 1977:1160).

General Introduction

§1. SWEDEN: A GENERAL BACKGROUND

1. Sweden is situated in northern Europe, between approximately the fifty-fifth and the seventieth parallels, in the southern and eastern parts of the Scandinavian Peninsula. Sweden covers 449,964 km^2, making it one of the largest countries in Europe. In relation to its size, the country's population, some 9.6 million, is fairly small. The capital of Sweden is Stockholm, which has about 1.3 million inhabitants.

Sweden is one of the northernmost countries in the world – it is situated at the same latitude as Kamchatka, Alaska, southern Greenland and also several polar areas. However, the proximity of the Atlantic Ocean gives it a much warmer climate than is found in Kamchatka and comparable locations, and no part of the country has a polar environment.

Sweden is covered to a large extent by forests; almost 10% of its area, however, consists of lakes and rivers. The southern areas of the country are largely agricultural. The present-day terrestrial and freshwater faunas found their way into Sweden after the last Ice Age; the southern parts of the country were inhabitable as recently as approximately 10,000 years ago.

2. Sweden has a relatively homogeneous population. The original Swedes belonged to Germanic tribes that came to the region by water to hunt and farm when the land became inhabitable again after the last Ice Age. During the Middle Ages, the western part of what is now Sweden was influenced by the nations on the western shores of the North Sea and the eastern part – including Stockholm – by the countries to the south of the Baltic Sea. Primarily during the seventeenth and eighteenth centuries, Sweden was involved to a large extent in the wars on the European continent, and these wars and matters connected with them meant that Sweden received a large influx of immigrants from other parts of Europe: Walloons to work in the mining and metalworking industries, Scots and Latvians to serve as soldiers, and so on. All these elements fused together quite well during the centuries to come. After the World War II, however, Sweden became an immigrant country. First came industrial workers, mainly from southern Europe, and later, from the beginning of the 1970s, refugees arrived from all over the world. Sweden is consequently far less homogeneous today than it was only a few decades ago.

3. Sweden has long been a democracy in the Western European tradition. It is also a monarchy, but the king – Carl XVI Gustaf (b. 1946) – now has only representative functions. In Sweden, the Speaker of Parliament is very high in the governing hierarchy, which shows the importance attached to Parliament.

General elections to the one-chamber Parliament take place every four years. Parliament alone has legislative power. The office of Parliamentary Ombudsman was created in Sweden by the Constitution of 1809, the first such office in the world.

The present Constitution dates from 1974.

4. The population, which is now 9.6 million, has grown almost fivefold since 1750, when national population registration was introduced. A large number of men and women cohabit without being married.

The birth rate is 11.6 per 1,000.

Employment by major group of economic activity in 2005 was as follows: farming, forestry, hunting and fishing: 39,000; manufacturing, electricity, gas and water: 628,000; construction: 225,000; trade in goods, restaurants and hotels: 567,000; communications: 247,000; finance and the like: 37,000; public administration and other services: 1,500,000.

5. The number of companies limited by shares (*aktiebolag* in Swedish) that were registered at the Companies Registration Office was 134,481 in 1984, 236,392 in 1989, 294,906 in 1993 and almost 310,000 at the end of 2005. Trading partnerships (*handelsbolag*) have also increased in number, from 15,765 on 1 January 1976 to 30,134 in 1979 and 76,573 in 1993. However, at the end of 2005, the number had decreased to 73,703. These figures include limited partnerships (*kommanditbolag*). The number of simple partnerships (*enkla bolag*) is uncertain.

6. Social and cultural values are shared to a very large degree by the people of Sweden. One reason for this is no doubt the fusion process described in paragraph 2 *supra*. Other reasons include the country's common language and its class structure, which is less pronounced than in most countries. Also important is that fact that the country has one main – though largely nominal – religion; most Swedes belong from their birth to their death to a Lutheran Church. The number of members of different religious denominations is, however, unknown.

7. A trend in modern Swedish society is for public services to be taken over to a large extent by private enterprises. The monopoly that the public sector had only a few decades ago in providing different kinds of services has now been appreciably reduced.

§2. The Historical Background of Companies and Partnerships

8. The first rules on partnerships in Sweden are found in certain medieval laws on, for example, farming partnerships and cooperation between a family and a partner outside the family. But these rules were few and inadequate. Hanseatic law was an early influence on partnerships for the purpose of trade. Later, Italian law indirectly influenced the law in Sweden through its direct influence of German law, as Swedish scholars introduced ideas from German law in Sweden. The liability of the partners of a trading partnership was accepted by Swedish law in a Royal Letter of 1673. Within the General Code of 1734, the trading partnership was devoted a chapter of its own – Chapter 15 – in the Commercial Code, where it was stated that each partner had the authority to represent the partnership in relation to third parties and that such representation made both the partnership and all partners personally and severally liable. This was the only form of partnership that was regulated in 1734, but other forms have survived besides the partnership proper – for example, the silent partnership.

Meanwhile, another form was developing without any legal regulation – namely, the company. The first Companies Act was not in fact put on the statute books until 1848.

The next move from the legislature came in 1895, when the chapter of the Commercial Code on partnerships was repealed and replaced by a new Act on partnerships, but this time not only trading partnerships, but also simple and limited partnerships were regulated. This legislation remained in force for more than eighty years; in 1980, a new Act – which is still in force – was adopted for these three forms of cooperation.

Also in 1895, the 1848 Companies Act was replaced by new legislation: the 1895 Companies Act. This Act was later replaced by new Companies Acts in 1910, 1944, 1975 and 2005, and the last of these acts is still in force in Sweden.

An Act on Cooperative Societies (*ekonomiska föreningar* in Swedish) was also adopted in 1895. This legislation has since been replaced by new enactments, in 1911, 1951 and 1987.

The remaining general forms of cooperation among natural and/or artificial persons or capital are non-profit member organizations (*ideella föreningar*) and foundations (*stiftelser*). There is no general legislation on non-profit member organizations. An Act on foundations was, however, put before the Swedish Parliament in 1993. It was adopted in 1994 and has been in force since 1 January 1996.

An Act on European Economic Interest Groupings (EEIGs) (*lag* 1994:1927 *om europeiska ekonomiska intressegrupperingar*) was adopted in 1994. It came into force on 1 January 1995.

§3. Definitions, Concepts and Structure of Companies and Partnerships

9. There are at least four different types of partnerships and companies in Sweden:

(1) *det enkla bolaget* (simple partnership);
(2) *handelsbolaget* (trading partnership);
(3) *kommanditbolaget* (limited partnership); and
(4) *aktiebolaget* (company limited by shares).

To these four types should perhaps be added *det tysta bolaget* (the silent partnership), a form that is characterized by the fact that one of the partners does business in his/her own name, with his/her co-partner(s) making his/her/their contribution(s) in such a way as to be invisible to anyone outside the partnership. Whether this form exists in Swedish law, however, is a question of some debate.

10. Until the end of 1994, there was only one form of *aktiebolag* in Sweden. In 1994, however, the forms of private and public companies were introduced. This reform, which took effect on 1 January 1995, was needed because of Sweden's participation in the European Economic Area (EEA) and the European Union's (EU's) demand for a higher share capital in ordinary companies than was previously required in Sweden (see further paragraphs 273 et seq. *infra*).

11. This presentation will concentrate on companies and trading partnerships, since these are the two main forms used for trading purposes. Some remarks will also be made, however, on simple and limited partnerships.

The basic form of partnership is the simple partnership (*det enkla bolaget*) – formerly the non-trading partnership. It is characterized by the fact that a number of persons – natural and/or artificial – have entered into an agreement to do something together for a common purpose and have all made or promised to make a contribution to the common purpose. This characterization is used as a means of drawing the line between partnerships, on the one hand, and loans, employer–employee relationships, landlord–tenant relationships, joint ownerships and the like, on the other. Simple partnerships are not legal persons.

A trading partnership was, until the end of 1994, characterized by the fact that two or more persons – natural and/or artificial – have entered into an agreement to do business in common in a partnership (as described in the preceding passage). This means that the line between simple and trading partnerships used to follow from whether business was carried on through the device of a partnership. Registration, which is now mandatory for trading partnerships, but not possible for simple partnerships as such, was until the end of 1994 generally of no importance in this connection. As of 1 January 1995, however, a trading partnership does not come into existence unless it is registered. Trading partnerships are legal persons.

Although a simple partnership is not a legal person and its members – the partners – are in principle not jointly liable for any debts, it can as of 1 January 1995 be used for enterprise purposes. The trading partnership, on the other hand, does business as such, and it is, as have already been stated, an enterprise with legal personality, but with joint liability for its partners. What has now been said about legal personality is also true of limited partnerships, but in these, some partners enjoy limited liability.

In Swedish terminology, both partnerships and companies limited by shares are called *bolag: enkelt bolag, handelsbolag, kommanditbolag, aktiebolag*. This means that in Sweden all these forms are deemed to belong to one 'family'. This might call for discussion of the line between the first three kinds of *bolag* – that is, those that are here called partnerships – and the last kind, the *aktiebolag*, the company limited by shares. This delimitation, however, very seldom causes any difficulty, since a company limited by shares cannot come into existence without being formed as such a company, and it also needs to be registered if it is to become an entity with legal personality whose members – the shareholders – are free from personal liability.

There are no bars built in by the legislature as to the degree to which the forms of partnership and company now mentioned may be used. A bar of another kind exists, however: The Swedish Companies Act is extensive, while the Partnerships Act – covering simple, trading and limited partnerships – is short and leaves many questions to be settled in the partnership agreement. People often prefer to know – or at least believe that they know – the answers to questions that might arise, and they therefore very often choose the company, with its stricter regulatory framework. In addition, tax considerations have led many people to choose the form of a company limited by shares.

12. Swedish law does not recognize any difference between commercial and civil law organizations.

13. In Swedish law, partnerships and companies are dealt with in the law of associations. This area of law also covers *ekonomiska föreningar* (cooperative societies) and *ideella föreningar* (non-profit member organizations). Closely connected to non-profit member organizations are *stiftelser* (foundations), which are organizations without any members. There is legislation covering *ekonomiska föreningar* and *stiftelser*, but no general Act governing *ideella föreningar*. Both kinds of *föreningar* and also *stiftelser* enjoy legal personality, although an *ekonomisk förening* does so only when it is registered. The members of *ekonomiska* and *ideella föreningar* are free from personal liability. These forms will not be dealt with in this book.

Finally, the rules of the Partnerships Act on *handelsbolag* (trading partnerships) are also applicable to mining partnerships to the degree that the Mining Act does not state otherwise. Neither *partrederier* (shipping partnerships) nor EEIGs will be dealt with here.

§4. Sources and Hierarchy of the Law on Companies and Partnerships

14. Legislation on partnerships has a long tradition in Sweden. As early a statute as the General Code of 1734 contained a chapter on partnerships, and this chapter was not repealed until 1895, when a new Act on the three different kinds of partnerships that are still found – the simple, trading and limited partnerships – was passed. This Act remained in force until the end of June 1981; then, on 1 July 1981, the 1980 Partnerships Act took effect. This Act is still in force.

The 1980 Partnerships Act is divided into four chapters. Chapter 1 contains five sections, of which only four is relevant here. The first section states when there is a trading partnership (see paragraph 11 *supra*), while the second section defines the limited partnership. The third states that a partnership that is not a trading partnership is a simple partnership, and the fourth states that trading and limited partnerships are entities with legal personality. The second chapter contains forty-six sections on trading partnerships, the third has eleven sections on limited partnerships and the fourth includes nine sections on simple partnerships.

Most sections concerning the relationship between the partners are non-compulsory, and that means that the content of the partnership agreement should be given the necessary thought. As for the relationship with third parties – who can represent and bind the partners or the partnership, who is liable, and so on – the rules are mandatory to a much higher degree. It should be added that partnerships sometimes exist without the partners being aware of the fact that they have formed a partnership. The question of whether a simple partnership exists or not is – as stated in paragraph 11 *supra* – dependent on the existence of certain constituting factors, not on the registration of something as a partnership.

A partnership, as I have already mentioned, is based on an agreement, a contract, and that means that ordinary contract rules can be used to settle questions on the binding effect of a partnership agreement.

Legislation on companies is in Sweden found in the 2005 Companies Act. This is the sixth Act on this topic, the first being from 1848 and the others from 1895, 1910, 1944 and 1975. The 1848 Act was based on French principles, but from 1895 onward, the influences have been stronger from Germany and, during the second part of the twentieth century, from England and the United States. This means that the Swedish legislation – in this as in many other fields of law – contains a mixture of ideas. Nevertheless, the basic structure comes from continental Europe. The Swedish company limited by shares still has a structure strongly reminiscent of what is found in Central Europe. But it also shows similarities with the legislation of the other Nordic countries.

The Swedish Companies Act 2005 is divided into thirty-two chapters, as compared with the 1975 Act, which contained only nineteen chapters. But even if the number of chapters and also the number of sections within them have increased, the basic ideas found in the legislation have not changed very much – the ideas on which earlier legislation in the area of companies was based have been brought forward under due observance of what EU directives demand.

To what degree the different sections of the Companies Act are mandatory or not is a question that is sometimes difficult to decide. A general rule, however, is that provisions that have as their only beneficiary the shareholders as such can, according to company law, be set aside if all the shareholders agree. Since Swedish company legislation accepts the one-man company, this means that wholly owned subsidiaries can be used to a large extent for the benefit of the parent company. But rules that have as their beneficiaries any third party have to be obeyed even in one-man companies.

Each company has to have its own articles of association stating, among other things, its name, where in Sweden the registered office of its board of directors is to be located (this will be the 'home' of the company), the kind of activity that the company is to engage in and its share capital or its maximum and minimum share capital.

The articles of association can be looked on as a kind of contract that is binding on all the members (shareholders) of the company.

General contract law can in principle also be applied to questions concerning company law. However, this will very rarely happen.

15. Other legislation than general contract law is of greater importance in connection with both partnerships and companies limited by shares. The Accounting Act of 1999 is applicable, for example, to trading partnerships, limited partnerships and companies. So, too, is the 1974 Business Names Act.

As to legislation that is applicable to trading and limited partnerships (but not to companies), mention should be made here of the 1974 Trade Registers Act. This Act states the obligation of – among others – trading and limited partnerships to register their name, the kind of activity they will carry on, the place where their main office will be situated as well as its postal address, the names and addresses of all the partners, by whom and how signature on behalf of the partnership is to take place when it is not performed by any one of the partners and, in the case of a limited partnership, which of the partners is not personally liable and the amount that such a partner has pledged.

§5. International Private Law

16. In Sweden, the general opinion is that entities that become legal persons through registration are subjects of the country in which they are registered (the incorporation theory). As to entities that are legal persons whether registered or not, the home of the board is decisive for the choice of law. If, however, the home of the board cannot be determined, the place where the entity's activities are mainly carried out is probably decisive.

§6. The Labour Law Connection: Codetermination and Corporate Structure

17. Trade unionism is strong in Sweden. Out of a population of somewhat more than 9.6 million, around 3.5 million are union members. The proportion of organized blue-collar workers has dropped to 66%, while the proportion of organized white-collar workers is approximately 73%.

Swedish legislation on trade unions builds to a very high degree on the unions that have concluded collective agreements with employers. These unions are usually referred to as established unions.

Collective agreements entered into are legally binding on the employer, the union, the members of the union at the moment when the agreement was concluded and also those who later become members (if they are not then bound by another collective agreement). Even if a member leaves the union, he/she will not cease to be bound by the agreement for the period for which it is in force. But normally the conditions of a collective agreement are also applied to outsiders at a plant whose work is covered by the agreement because such an agreement normally includes an express or implied obligation on the employer – in relation to the established union – not to offer other employment conditions than those applicable to union members.

The established trade unions influence the decisions made by companies and sometimes also by partnerships in various ways.

The 1987 Act on Board Representation for Employees in the Private Sector states in its first section that the purpose of the Act is to guarantee employees insight into and influence over the activities of – among others – companies limited by shares (but not partnerships). This insight and influence, however, are not given to the employees as such, but to the established unions. The latter have the right to appoint two representatives on the board of any company with twenty-five or more employees; if the number of employees is 1,000 or more and the company has activities in different branches of trade and industry, the number of union appointed directors is three. The number of union representatives on the board, however, may not exceed the number of directors elected by other means. It is not intended that the union members of the board should be in a majority (unless the company is owned by the union, which is another matter). Union directors are normally bound by the same rules as other directors. Some exceptions exist, however. Deputy union directors are given a mandatory right to attend and take part in discussions at a board meeting even if the regular director is attending the meeting. Furthermore, one of the union directors has the right to participate in the work of a committee with the task of preparing business that is later to be discussed at a board meeting. Finally, union directors are barred from being present when the board discusses issues that concern collective agreements, industrial action (lockouts, strikes, etc.) or other matters where any trade union at the plant has an essential interest that may be contrary to that of the company.

The following acts are applicable to all employers, including both companies and partnerships.

An important piece of legislation is the 1976 Act on Codetermination in Working Life. This Act confers on the established unions several rights that are of great importance to them and their members. Thus, before an employer decides on an important alteration to his activities, he must, on his own initiative, negotiate with the established union(s). And the same requirement must be observed before he decides on important changes in the work or employment conditions of employees belonging to such a union. (If urgent reasons so necessitate, the employer may, however, make and implement a decision before he has fulfilled his duty to negotiate with the union.) The employer may be under an obligation to negotiate with the established union(s) in other situations, too, if the union so requests. However, an employer not bound by a collective agreement must negotiate with all trade unions present at the company before a decision concerning dismissal due to redundancy is made, as well as before making a decision of transferring the company's activities. An employer is, furthermore, required to keep the established union(s) continuously informed about how his operations are developing in terms of production as well as financially and about guidelines on personnel policy. The employer must, additionally, afford the union an opportunity to examine books, accounts and other documents concerning his activities to the extent that the organization needs such access in order to take care of its members' common interests in relation to the employer. The employer, however, if he deems it necessary, has the right to negotiate with the union over a duty of confidentiality with respect to information that he has to furnish. An employer not bound by a collective agreement must negotiate with all trade unions at the company before a decision concerning dismissal due to redundancy or transfer to another company is decided.

Furthermore, the Act states that the parties to a collective agreement 'should' also conclude a collective agreement on the right of employees to take part in decisions concerning the conclusion and termination of employment contracts, the direction and distribution of work and the conduct of the employer's activities in other respects – in short, all aspects of management. The desideratum pronounced by the Act – *should* – is backed up by a special right for the established unions to strike if no such collective agreement on joint regulation is forthcoming. It should be added that where a dispute arises over the application of an agreement of the kind now discussed or over the duty of a member of an established union to perform work under a collective agreement, the union's view shall, in principle, apply until the dispute is finally tried. On the other hand, where a legal dispute arises over wages or other remuneration for a member of an established union, it is the duty of the employer to immediately call for negotiations in relation to the dispute if the employer is not willing to pay what the union demands. If the dispute cannot be resolved through negotiations, he has to bring an action before the Labour Court. Finally, in relation to the Codetermination Act, in certain situations the established unions have the right to veto the use of the services of persons who are not employed by the employer.

Unions exercise influence on behalf of members and non-members under other statutes, too, such as the Vacations Act, the Security of Employment Act, the Educational Leave Act, the Working Environment Act, the Act on the Position of Trade Union Representatives at the Workplace, the Working Time Act, the Employment Protection Act and the Act on Litigation in Labour Disputes.

In addition, it should be noted that Sweden has, like other European countries, been influenced by EU directives in the area of labour law.

Part I. Companies

Chapter 1. Companies Limited by Shares

18. As noted in the Introduction, there are – in addition to the *Societas Europea* (SE) which will be dealt with later (paragraph 285 *infra*) – two main kinds of share companies in Sweden, private and public companies. All companies are nevertheless formed under and, with few exceptions, have to follow the same rules. The main differences concern the minimum share capital and the right of the company and its shareholders to turn to the public for financial resources. The minimum share capital of a private company is SEK 50,000 and of a public company SEK 500,000 (or, in both cases, the equivalent amount in EUR), and only public companies and their shareholders may turn to the public to obtain financial resources. Thus, according to the Companies Act, Chapter 1, section 7, a private company or a shareholder in such a company may not, through advertising, attempt to sell shares or subscription rights in the company or debentures or warrants issued by the company. Nor may a private company or a shareholder in such a company otherwise attempt to sell such securities by offering them for subscription or sale to an open group, which in most cases means a group of no more than 200 persons. This shall not, however, apply where the offer is directed solely to a group of persons who have previously given notice of interest in such offers and where no more than 200 trading units are offered. These prohibitions shall, further, not apply to offers that relate to transfers to not more than ten purchasers. Nor shall the prohibitions apply to companies with special limitations on dividends (see paragraphs 263 et seq. *infra* concerning such companies).

The shares of public companies and other financial instruments may, *a contrario*, be sold and bought on the securities market.

19. If the shareholders of a public company wish it to become a private company, this has to be decided at a general meeting of the company. A proposal to change the status of the company from public to private is not adopted unless all the shareholders present at the meeting have accepted the proposal and, in addition, these shareholders represent nine-tenths of the shares of the company (see further the Companies Act, Chapter 26, section 6). If, on the other hand, the shareholders of a private company wish it to become a public company, this is decided by the general meeting as a normal amendment of the articles of association (see Chapter 26, section 1).

The differences between private and public companies are treated in some detail in paragraphs 273 et seq. *infra*.

§1. Formation

20. The formation of a company is regulated in Chapter 2 of the Companies Act.

I. One-Man Companies

21. As was noted in the Introduction to this book, the one-man company is accepted in Swedish law. The legislature took this position as early as 1944, knowing that a requirement that there be several shareholders would not be a real hindrance when one person – natural or artificial – wished to carry on business activities without assuming personal liability. Now and then this could be done quite openly, but in most cases, the real shareholder would transfer one or more shares to the number of persons required. These persons would sometimes be owners only in the formal sense of the word, and it is generally impossible to decide when a shareholder is a fictitious shareholder and when he/she is not. In its 1941 report (leading to the Act of 1944), the Companies Act Committee expressed the opinion that it would not preserve the dignity of the legislation to maintain a legal state in which rules that were regarded as being among the main provisions of the legislation could be set aside – generally without any sanction. Furthermore, the Committee said, removing the right of fictitious shareholders to hold shares could cause serious changes in the assumed rights and obligations of existing companies with such shareholders. Besides, the risk to the creditors of a company and other third parties could often be presumed to be just as great in companies with one principal shareholder and additional real shareholders cooperating harmoniously with him/her as in companies with only one shareholder. Finally, there could be quite legitimate reasons why a person should want to transfer a part of his/her fortune to a legal entity. The form of a limited company could be useful not only when the aim was to attract capital from a large number of interested parties, but also when starting a particularly risky business or when the purpose is to achieve organizational improvements. Economic development would be hindered if a party were not allowed to invest a part of his/her fortune in a risky, but as it might later turn out, important business. The essential thing was that the share capital – the security of the creditors – be safeguarded to the highest possible degree. That the form of a one-man company could offer significant organizational advantages had been shown by the strong trend towards more and more subsidiaries during the two or three decades immediately preceding the reform of the law.

II. Founders

22. Despite the fact that the 1944 Companies Act accepted the one-man company, three persons were still required as founders. This was changed in 1975, with Chapter 2, section 1, of the then new Act stating that a company is formed by one or more founders. And this is still so (see Chapter 2, section 1 of the 2005 Companies Act). Consequently, all shares may be subscribed for by one person. A company is founded by one or more natural or legal person(s) (Chapter 1, section 1).

However, a person who is under age – that is, is not yet 18 years old – or is in bankruptcy or has a custodian according to the rules of the Parental Code may not be a founder. Nor may a person who has been declared subject to an incapacity to engage in trade be a founder (Chapter 2, section 2).

III. Share Capital

23. The initial share capital must be at least SEK 50,000 in a private company and at least SEK 500,000 in a public company (or, in both cases, the equivalent amount in EUR). The amount stated in the Companies Act is just the minimum. The founder(s) can choose whatever amount he/she/they wish as long as it is at least SEK 50,000 or SEK 500,000, respectively. Where the share capital is divided into several shares, all shares represent an equal part of the share capital.

Either the share capital or the minimum and the maximum share capital must be stated in the articles of association (see paragraph 26 *infra*). The latter alternative is very common in Sweden, since it allows considerable scope to change the actual share capital without first amending the articles of association.

IV. Formation Conditions

24. The Companies Act states in Chapter 2, section 3, how a new company is founded. The founder(s) shall prepare a draft memorandum of association; one or more founders shall subscribe for all shares in the company; the shares shall be paid for; the founders(s) shall prepare, date and sign the memorandum of association; and the board of directors shall apply for registration of the company at the Companies Registration Office.

The draft memorandum of association shall (Chapter 2, section 5) stipulate the conditions for the formation of the company, among them a provision regarding the amount to be paid for each share, which may not be fixed at less than the quota value of the share. The price may, on the other hand, be more than the quota value. In this case, the difference is allocated to the share premium reserve. Where a share may be subscribed for with a right or an obligation to contribute property other than cash as payment for the share, the value of that property may not be fixed at a higher amount than its real value to the company. Property other than cash may consist only of property that benefits or that is expected to benefit the operations of the company. An obligation to perform work for or render services to the company may not be used as a contribution of property other than cash (Chapter 2, section 6).

The draft memorandum of association shall also state the full names of (and also other information on) the members of the board of directors and, where relevant, auditors and, where appropriate, deputy directors, deputy auditors and general examiners.

The draft memorandum of association shall further, where appropriate, state *if* subscription for a share may take place subject to a right or obligation of the company to takeover property in exchange for shares or for compensation other than shares, *if* subscription for a share may take place subject to other rights or conditions and *if* the company shall reimburse costs incurred in the formation of the company (Chapter 2, section 5, paragraph 2)

The draft memorandum of association shall always include articles of association for the proposed company (Chapter 2, section 10).

Where a public company is formed, the memorandum of association shall contain information regarding all costs associated with the formation of the company (Chapter 2, section 28).

V. Procedure

25. Traditionally, the formation of a company was a rather formalized procedure.

Such a procedure was deemed to be a safeguard both for those who wished to subscribe for shares and for other third parties. The formalities have, however, been reduced in the 2005 Companies Act.

The 1975 Companies Act distinguished between simultaneous and successive formation. The latter kind of formation was used when outsiders were invited to subscribe for shares. According to the 2005 Companies Act, outsiders are, however, never invited to subscribe for shares; consequently, the only kind of formation accepted in the new Act is simultaneous formation.

The idea behind the existing regulation is to prevent the use of the form of a company limited by shares in such a way that any third party may be harmed. What the Act tries to ensure is that a new company has an economic base that is – if not sufficient, because that is something that the legislature cannot achieve as such – at any rate as safe as the founders state and that third parties are as far as possible able to trust that a registered company has the economic base that it is said to have.

Therefore, one or more founders shall subscribe for all the shares in the company. The subscription shall take place in the memorandum of association. The subscription is binding on the subscriber when the memorandum of association has been signed by all the founders (Chapter 2, section 12).

If a share has been subscribed for on terms that do not accord with the memorandum of association, the subscriber is not able to invoke such terms. And following the registration of the company, a share subscriber may not claim, as ground for invalidity of the share subscription that any of the terms of the memorandum of association has not been fulfilled (Chapter 2, section 14).

The payment for a share may not be less than the share's quota value (Chapter 2, section 15).

As already mentioned, payment in cash shall take place through deposit in a separate account opened by the founders for such purpose (Chapter 2, section 17). As to payment with non-cash consideration, an auditor must provide a written, signed statement to the effect (1) that all non-cash consideration has been conveyed to the company; (2) that the non-cash consideration is, or may be assumed to be, for the benefit of the company's operations; and (3) that the non-cash consideration has not been reported in the memorandum of association at a higher value than the actual value for the company (Chapter 2, section 19).

A debt resulting from share subscription may not be set off against a claim against the company (Chapter 2, section 21).

When the draft memorandum of association has been prepared, the founder(s) has (have) subscribed for the shares, the shares have been paid for and the founder(s) has (have) dated and signed the memorandum of association, then the company is founded (Chapter 2, section 4), and the members of the board of directors and, where relevant, auditors and, where appropriate, deputy members of the board of directors, deputy auditors and general examiners – all mentioned in the draft memorandum of association (see paragraph 24 *supra*) – start to function. The company is, however, not yet a legal person (see VII *infra*)

26. The memorandum of association shall include articles of association. These articles will become the 'basic law' of the company/the basic agreement between the shareholders.

The articles of association are required (Chapter 3, section 1) to specify at least the following points:

(1) the business name of the company;
(2) the location in Sweden of the registered office of the board of directors;
(3) the activity of the company, stating the kind thereof;
(4) the share capital or, where it may be fixed at a lower or higher level without amendment of the articles of association, the minimum and the maximum share capital, the minimum capital to be not less than one-fourth of the maximum capital;
(5) the number of shares or, where a minimum share capital and a maximum share capital are stated in the articles of association, a minimum and maximum of the number of shares, it being stipulated that the relation between the minimum capital and the lowest number of shares shall be the same as the relation between the maximum capital and the highest number of shares;
(6) the number, or the minimum and the maximum numbers, of board directors;
(7) the number, or the minimum and the maximum numbers, of deputy directors, where such shall be appointed;
(8) the number, or the minimum and maximum numbers, of auditors where such shall be appointed;
(9) the procedure for convening general meetings; and
(10) the financial year of the company.

Where the business name of a public company does not include the word *publikt* – that is, public – the letters (*publ*) shall be added to the name of the company in the articles of association (Chapter 3, section 11).

The provisions of points 6 and 7 on directors and deputy directors do not bear on employee representatives appointed in accordance with the 1987 Act on Board Representation for Employees in the Private Sector.

Small private companies have as of 1 November 2010 been given the right to refrain from having any auditors.

VI. Registration

27. An application for registration of the company at the Companies Registration Office is required (Chapter 2, sections 22 and 24) to be submitted within six months of the signing of the memorandum of association, failing which the formation of the company will lapse.

Registration is barred unless (1) the total of the minimum amounts that are to be paid for the subscribed shares (the company's share capital) corresponds to the share capital stated in the articles of association or amounts to not less than the minimum capital; (2) full and acceptable payment has been made for all subscribed shares; (3) a certificate is produced concerning payments in cash; (4) an auditor's statement is produced concerning non-cash consideration and such obligations for the company as stated in the memorandum of association; and (5) the formation of the company has otherwise taken place pursuant to the Companies Act and other statutory instruments (Chapter 2, section 23).

The Companies Registration Office is required to announce entries in the Companies Register without delay in the Official Gazette.

28. Certain acquisitions of property from founders or shareholders made within two years of the date of registration of a public company are to be approved by the general meeting (Chapter 2, section 29). If the contract is approved, it must be registered immediately (Chapter 2, section 31).

VII. Legal Personality

29. By registration, the company becomes a legal person and, as such, can acquire rights, assume obligations and be party to legal actions before courts or other authorities (Chapter 2, section 25).

Although the company becomes a legal person upon registration, before registration takes place the board of directors may institute legal actions regarding the formation of the company and take other steps to collect subscribed amounts or other promised contributions.

Where an obligation is assumed by an action on behalf of the company prior to its registration, those who have taken part in or decided on that action are jointly and severally liable for the obligation. Upon registration, the liability passes to the company, however, provided it results from the draft memorandum of association or has arisen after the foundation of the company (Chapter 2, section 26).

Where an agreement made on behalf of the company has been entered into prior to registration with a party who knew that the company was not registered, that party may, unless the agreement provides otherwise, withdraw from it if an application for registration has not been submitted within the time limit prescribed in the Companies Act – that is, six months after the signing of the memorandum of association – or the Companies Registration Office, by a decision no longer subject to appeal, has dismissed the application or refused registration of the company. Where, however, the party did not know that the company was not registered, he/she may withdraw from the agreement also prior to registration of the company (Chapter 2, section 27).

30. The shareholders of a company that has become a legal person bear no personal liability for the company's obligations as long as there is no deficiency in the share capital (Chapter 1, section 3). See paragraph 95 *infra* concerning liability in such situations.

VIII. Miscellaneous

31. As has already been mentioned in paragraph 26 *supra*, the articles of association must include the business name of the company, the location in Sweden of the registered office of the board of directors, and the kind of activity that the company is to be engaged in.

32. Regarding the business name of the company, Chapter 28 of the Companies Act makes certain stipulations, such as that the name must contain the word *aktiebolag* or the abbreviation *AB*, that the name must be clearly distinguishable from other names previously entered and still registered in the Companies Register or the Register of Branches and that in other respects the provisions of the Business Names Act shall apply to the registration of the company. Where a name is to be registered in two or several languages, each version must be stated in the articles of association.

The letters *(publ)* must be added to the business name of a public company unless the business name itself indicates that the company is public (Chapter 28, section 7). No letters are added to the business name of a private company.

33. The location in Sweden of the board of directors is the place where, normally, the general meeting is to be held. This location is also decisive as to jurisdiction relating to the company.

34. Every Swedish company has a registration number (according to the Act of 1974 on Identification Designations for Artificial Persons, etc.). This number follows each company during its entire existence and makes it possible to identify a company even if it has changed its business name.

35. A company's letterhead, invoices, order forms and usually websites shall state the business name of the company and the location of the registered office of the directors, as well as the company's registration number. Where the company has gone into liquidation, such fact shall also be stated (Chapter 28, section 5).

Written documents to be executed on behalf of the company should state the business name of the company, as the person(s) signing the document may otherwise incur personal liability (Chapter 28, section 6).

36. The kind of activity that the company is to be engaged in should be distinguished from the purpose of the company, which normally is to make profits for its shareholders. Only if the purpose of the company's activities is, wholly or partly, other than making profits for the shareholders are the articles of association required to contain provisions on how the profits and the remaining assets in connection with the winding-up of the company are to be used (see Chapter 3, section 3). Such a clause can later be amended if the shareholders so decide.

However, the Companies Act also contains a chapter on companies with special limitations on dividends that allows companies to be formed for mandatory non-profit purposes. In such companies, amendment of the articles of association in order to change their non-profit character will not be possible (see further paragraphs 263 et seq. *infra*).

The activities of a company, on the other hand, must always be stated in some detail in the articles of association. The idea behind this rule is that the shareholders should know the kind of activities that the company is allowed to engage in. Vague descriptions are thus not permitted: Registration of 'trading activity' or 'industrial activity' will not be allowed. But neither is too much specialization to be recommended, since the articles bind the general meeting and those working in and for the company and amendment of the articles would take some time if a change of activity were to prove necessary.

The activities of the company can normally be of any kind – not only commercial, industrial or other business activities, but also, for example, information activities and other activities of an idealistic nature. Limitations may nevertheless follow from other legislation.

37. Any document that, pursuant to the Companies Act, must be signed may, unless otherwise stated, be signed by using an advanced electronic signature pursuant to the Qualified Electronic Signatures Act (Chapter 1, section 13).

38. The text *infra* refers now and then to central securities depository (CSD) companies. In such companies, the articles of association contain a clause stating that the company's shares shall be registered in a CSD register pursuant to the 1998 Financial Instruments (Accounts) Act (Chapter 1, section 10). See further paragraphs 118 et seq. *infra*.

§2. Capital and Shares

I. Introduction

39. As noted above, the articles of association state the share capital or, if so decided, the minimum and the maximum share capital. The minimum share capital is SEK 50,000 for a private company and SEK 500,000 for a public company. If the minimum-maximum alternative is used, it is possible to change the share capital within the minimum-maximum limits without any amendment of the articles of association.

If the share capital is divided into several shares, each share has the same quota value.

As also noted earlier, the amount to be paid for each share may not be fixed at less than the quota value. The amount may, on the other hand, be fixed at more than the quota value. Any amount paid over and above the quota value shall be recorded in the share premium reserve.

Property other than cash (capital contributed in kind) is, as we have seen, allowed on two conditions: Its value may not be fixed at a higher amount than its real value to the company, and it may consist only of property that benefits or is expected to benefit the company. An obligation to perform work for or to render services to the company may never be accepted as property other than cash.

Offset against a claim for subscription of shares is not allowed at this stage in the 'life' of a company (Chapter 2, section 21).

What has been subscribed for must be paid for in full before registration can take place. Where the subscribed amount is paid in cash, the payment has to be deposited in a bank account that the founder(s) has (have) opened for this purpose with a bank, a credit market undertaking or an equivalent foreign credit institution in a state within the EEA (Chapter 2, section 17). The bank issues a certificate stating the amount that has been paid into the account. This certificate has to be enclosed with the application for registration.

Property other than cash must, as was also noted above, be contributed in full before registration can take place. In this case, an auditor has to issue a statement certifying that the property has been transferred to the company, that the property has not been given a higher value in the memorandum of association than its real value to the company and that the property benefits or may be expected to benefit the activities of the company.

Certain acquisitions of property from founders or shareholders that have taken place within two years of the registration of a public company have to be approved by the general meeting (Chapter 2, sections 29–31).

40. When a duly registered company starts its activities, the share capital is rarely enough. Usually, the company also needs other resources. These resources may be obtained by borrowing from banking institutions and other third parties.

The Companies Act has some rules concerning loan capital, but more on shareholders' equity. According to the Act, equity is divided into two groups, restricted and non-restricted. Restricted equity is characterized by the fact that dividends and other payments to the shareholders (in their capacity as shareholders) are forbidden unless the restricted equity is left intact. It is therefore important to know which equity is restricted. Restricted equity consists of the share capital, the revaluation reserve, the statutory (legal) reserve and the equity method reserve (the Annual Reports Act 1995, Chapter 5, section 14). The articles of association may – but very seldom do – add rules on restricted equity.

Non-restricted equity, on the other hand, may in principle be distributed to the shareholders.

Interest has to be paid on loan capital, and the capital might have to be amortized. Whether the shareholders will be paid any dividend depends on the financial result of the company, and reduction in the share capital involving repayment to the shareholders must follow the rules of the Companies Act. Therefore, a company in need of more capital for its activities might prefer to increase its share capital.

Before we go into the matter of increasing the share capital through a new issue, however, two points should be noted:

(1) It might be difficult for a company to find persons willing to subscribe for new shares. Therefore, the Companies Act contains rules on warrants and convertible instruments. These alternatives combine to a certain extent the advantages of shares and loans. We will come back to them in paragraphs 136 et seq. *infra.*
(2) The share capital may also be increased without any payment for new shares – that is, a bonus issue can take place.

II. Increasing the Share Capital

A. *Bonus Issues*

41. A bonus issue may, according to the Companies Act (Chapter 12, section 1), be effected by transferring to the share capital amounts that are free for distribution to the shareholders according to the latest adopted balance sheet or amounts from the statutory (legal) reserve or the revaluation reserve or by revaluing fixed assets (according to conditions stated in the 1995 Annual Reports Act). In reality, a bonus issue is nothing but an accounting transaction.

A resolution to increase the share capital by a bonus issue usually has to be adopted by a simple majority at a general meeting of the shareholders. Where the articles of association need to be amended, a resolution to this effect must first be adopted by a qualified majority (the Companies Act 2005, Chapter 11, section 2 and Chapter 7, section 42).

Shareholders have, according to Chapter 12, section 2, a preferential right to the new shares in a bonus issue in relation to the number of shares they already own unless the articles of association provide otherwise by stipulating that the shares do not carry equal rights to participate in the company's assets or profits. If the old shares belong to different classes concerning, for example, voting rights, new shares of each class shall be issued in relation to the number of shares of the same class that are already issued.

The Companies Act states in Chapter 12, sections 4–7, what information the shareholders must receive before the decision may be made and, in Chapter 12, section 8, that the board of directors shall make the proposed bonus issue resolution available to the shareholders during a period of not less than two weeks before the general meeting where the proposal is to be considered and that copies of the documents shall be sent to the shareholders who so request and state their addresses. In public companies with their shares listed on a regulated market or an equivalent market outside the EEA, the period during which the proposed resolution shall be made available is however extended to three weeks and it must also be published at the website of the company (Chapter 12, section 8).

Notification for registration of the resolution on a bonus issue must be submitted without delay to the Companies Registration Office (Chapter 12, section 10).

B. New Issues

1. General Conditions

42. Let us now turn to increases in the share capital through new issues.

The problems connected with this kind of issue are to some extent the same as those discussed in connection with formation of a company, and the solutions contained in Chapter 13 – which deals with new issues – are to some degree the same as those in the chapter on the founding of companies. But sometimes the problems are different or at least solved differently.

43. A resolution to increase the share capital has to be adopted at a general meeting of the shareholders unless either the board of directors decides on a new issue *subject to approval* by the general meeting (Chapter 13, sections 31–34) or the general meeting has *authorized the board* of directors to make such an issue (sections 35–38) (see paragraph 46 *infra*). The latter alternative presupposes both that the new issue can be effected without amending the articles of association – that is, that the articles of association state a minimum-maximum share capital – and that the board makes the decision within a period that may not extend beyond the opening of the next ordinary general meeting of shareholders.

Where the articles of association need to be amended, a resolution to this effect must be passed before a resolution to increase the share capital may be adopted. Such a decision requires a qualified majority.

44. The board of directors or the person proposing the new issue has to make a proposal for the increase in the capital according to what is stated in Chapter 13, sections 4–7.

If the shares are not to be paid for in cash, the shares may be paid for both by property other than cash and, if either the issue resolution contains a provision thereon or the company is a public company and it is allowed according to what is stated in Chapter 13, section 41, by way of setoff.

The amount to be paid for each share may in principle not be fixed at less than the quota value of the share. Very often, it is fixed at a higher amount than the quota value. In the latter case, the extra amount is allocated to the share premium reserve. The words 'in principle' refer to a rule (Chapter 13, section 4) that is applicable only to companies whose shares are traded on a regulated market or an equivalent market outside the EEA. A new issue in such companies may be subscribed for on payment of less than quota value, provided that the difference between the amount to be paid for the new shares and their quota value is added to the share capital by a transfer from other equity of the company or by a revaluation of fixed assets. This rule was added to the 1975 Companies Act in 1980 – at a time when the market quotation of shares was often below their quota value and when, without a rule like the one just presented, new issues were impossible because of the demand that at least the quota value be paid. What this rule in fact makes possible is a combined new and bonus issue. But the legislature has not dared to give the right to use this device to companies other than those whose shares are traded on a regulated or equivalent market.

Where a share may be subscribed for with a right or an obligation to contribute property other than cash as payment or with a right or an obligation for the company to takeover property for other consideration than shares, the value of that property may not be fixed at a higher amount than its real value for the company. Property other than cash may further consist only of property that benefits or is expected to benefit the operations of the company. Where a share is subscribed for on a condition that is contrary to what has thus been stipulated, the quota value shall still be paid (Chapter 13, sections 7 and 8).

45. The amount to be paid for subscribed shares is usually lower than the official quotation or the market value of the shares in the company. The new issue is likely to succeed only if the subscription price is favourable to those who are invited to subscribe. This means that the right to subscribe has an economic value. In addition, the majority–minority relationship can change if the shareholders are not given a right to subscribe in relation to the number of shares that they already own. Therefore, the Companies Act proceeds from the assumption that the shareholders of a company have a preferential right to new shares in relation to the number of shares that they own at the time when the decision to increase the capital is made. Nevertheless, the Act states that the preferential right of the existing shareholders can be set aside because either (1) the shares will be paid for with non-cash consideration or (2) the pre-emption right will be governed in another manner as a consequence of (a) such provisions of the articles of association as are referred to in Chapter 4, section 3 (see paragraph 97 *infra*), (b) conditions that have been issued in conjunction of an earlier issue of warrants or convertible instruments (see paragraphs 138 et seq. and 146 et seq. *infra*) or (c) provisions of the issue resolution (Chapter 13, section 1). A decision to set aside the preferential right requires in the last case (i.e., point (c)) a majority of at least two-thirds both of the votes cast and of the shares represented at the meeting (see Chapter 13, section 2). When a public company or a subsidiary to such a company decides to direct the issue to the categories mentioned in paragraph 47 *infra*, that decision needs the support of nine-tenths both of the votes and of the shares represented at the meeting (Chapter 16, section 8).

If the new issue is to be paid for with property other than cash or by setoff of claims against the company (i.e., case 1 *supra*), only those who own the property or have the claims can, of course, be given the right to subscribe. However, if this right (to pay for new issues with other property than money) is used in a way that gives an undue benefit to the subscriber and a disfavour of other shareholders or the company, the action will not be in keeping with the general clause (see paragraph 48 *infra*).

2. Authorization for the Board

46. An authorization for the board of directors to decide on a new issue (see paragraph 43 *supra*) must state, for example, if the authorization is *either* to include the right to provide for the contribution of non-cash property or the right to set off the cost against claims on the company or to stipulate that the board shall be entitled to derogate from the shareholders' preferential rights (Chapter 13, sections 35 and 36).

This special authorization is decided on at the general meeting by a simple majority, except when the board is to be authorized to deviate from the shareholders' preferential rights. Then the Act requires a two-thirds majority both of the votes cast and of the shares represented at the meeting.

47. The board may never, however, use an authorization to direct a new issue of shares (or an issue of warrants or convertible instruments) in a public company or a subsidiary of such a company to board directors, managing directors and other employees of the company or other companies within the same group; to spouses or co-habitants of or children under age in the care of directors, managing directors or employees; or to legal persons over which persons in the categories mentioned have a determining influence. Issues of shares (and other issues) in which existing shareholders' preferential rights were bypassed were a common way to favour the interests of persons inside a company at the expense of the ordinary shareholders. In reality, this was often done in violation of certain general provisions of the Companies Act, and the rule forbidding directed share (and other) issues in public companies by the board was in 1987 set out in a separate Act, the 1987 Act on Directed Issues in Stock Market Companies, etc. These rules are, however, now incorporated in Chapter 16 of the 2005 Companies Act. However, if the Stock Market Company is listed on a regulated market, even harder rules will be applicable due to the registration contract.

For private companies, the general rules of the Companies Act are to be followed.

3. Minority Protection

48. The Companies Act contains two clauses that can be invoked in case the decisions in a company are seriously damaging the interests of the shareholders – for example, if a new issue should be directed in an unacceptable way. These clauses, referred to as the *general clauses* in the Companies Act, are found in Chapter 8, section 41, and Chapter 7, section 47. They state that neither the board of directors nor other representatives of the company nor the general meeting may enter into legal transactions, undertake other measures or pass resolutions that are likely to give undue advantage to a shareholder or third party to the detriment of the company or other shareholders. These clauses were in fact added to the Companies Act in their present form when the right to direct share issues paid for in cash was first introduced in Sweden (1973) as a means of restraining the use of directed issues in situations where they were not in accordance with the ideas of the legislature. During the more than forty years that these clauses have been in force, they have rarely been invoked at court, but they have probably had some effect as signposts.

4. Procedure

49. A draft resolution to increase the share capital by a new issue, to be decided on by the general meeting, must (under Chapter 13, sections 4–8), together with all relevant documents, be made available to the shareholders for not less than two weeks before the general meeting at which it is to be adopted and also must immediately be sent to any shareholder who requests it and informs the company of his/her mailing address. The documents shall also be presented to the general meeting. – In public companies with their shares listed on a regulated market or an equivalent market outside the EEA, the period during which the proposed resolution shall be made available is however extended to three weeks and it must also be published at the website of the company.

The resolution must normally specify (Chapter 13, section 4) *inter alia* (1) the amount or the maximum amount by which the share capital can be increased or the minimum and maximum amounts of the increase; (2) the number of shares, the maximum number of shares or the minimum number of shares to be issued; (3) the amount to be paid for each new share; (4) the right to subscribe for shares that vests in the shareholders or any third party; (5) the period of time within which subscription for shares shall take place; (6) the allotment principle to be applied by the board of directors with respect to shares not subscribed for pursuant to pre-emption rights; (7) the period of time within which payment shall be made for shares or, where appropriate, within which subscription through payment pursuant to Chapter 13, section 13, shall take place; and (8) the date from which the new shares shall carry a right to dividend.

Where the proposal entails derogation from the shareholders' pre-emption rights, the reasons for such derogation and the principles on which the subscription price is based shall be stated in the proposal or in an appended document.

The resolution must also contain the provisions covering the contribution of non-cash property, the right to use setoff claims against the company and any other conditions for the subscription (Chapter 13, sections 5–7). The Act goes into detail on what information must be included in or attached to the report concerning the assessment of the value of such property.

When the general meeting has made its decision, the resolution shall, in companies that are not CSD companies, immediately be distributed to the shareholders that hold pre-emption rights to participate in the issue – unless they were all represented at the general meeting at which the resolution was adopted, in which Case No such distribution is necessary (Chapter 13, section 12).

50. After the decision to increase the share capital is made, the subscription of new shares and the allotment of new shares follow. If the new issue has been successful, the new shares have to be paid for. Payment in cash to a private company shall take place through deposit in a separate account opened by the company for such purpose (Chapter 13, section 21). However, in a public company, the payment for the new shares may, alternatively, be paid directly to the company (Chapter 13, section 40). As to payment with non-cash consideration, an auditor must – in private as well as in public companies (Chapter 13, sections 23 and 42) – provide a written, signed statement to the effect (1) that all non-cash consideration has been conveyed to the company; (2) that the non-cash consideration is, or may be assumed to be, of benefit for the company's operations; and (3) that the non-cash consideration has not been reported in the proposal at a higher value than the actual value for the company. A debt as a consequence of subscription for shares may in a private company be set off against a claim on the company only where the issue resolution contains a provision thereon. In a public company, a set off against a claim on the company is also possible in other situations (Chapter 13, section 41).

51. If a share has been subscribed for on a condition that is contrary to the resolution, the subscription is invalid. If the Companies Registration Office has not been notified of the invalidity prior to the registration of the issue, the subscriber is bound by his/her subscription, but not allowed to invoke the condition (Chapter 13, section 16).

52. When the subscription has been completed, the board of directors decides on the allotment of new shares among the subscribers (Chapter 13, section 18).

53. Where a certain amount or a minimum amount has been fixed for the increase in the share capital and this amount has not been subscribed for within the prescribed period, the resolution on the issue becomes void. The same applies to a resolution to amend the articles of association that presupposes an increase in the share capital (Chapter 13, section 17).

5. Registration

54. An application for registration of the resolution on a new issue is required (Chapter 13, section 27) to be submitted to the Companies Registration Office within six months from the date of the resolution unless it has become void in the manner described in paragraph 53 *supra.* In private companies registration is barred unless:

(1) the total of the amounts that are to be paid for subscribed and allotted shares equals the amount or minimum amount by which the company's share capital is to be increased through the issue;
(2) full and acceptable payment has been provided for all subscribed and allotted shares;
(3) a certificate is presented regarding payment in cash; and
(4) an auditor's statement is presented regarding non-cash consideration as stated in the issue resolution.

III. Public Issue Requirements

A. The Companies Act

55. When the 2005 Companies Act was passed in the summer of 2005, it still included rules on prospectuses. However, these rules were annulled before the Companies Act became effective – that is, when the Financial Instruments Trading Act was amended in the late 2005. The only rules in the 2005 Companies Act on prospectuses and other public issues are now those in Chapter 29, sections 1 and 2, which state that board members, managing directors and auditors are liable in damages for violation of the rules in the Financial Instruments Trading Act on prospectuses, public takeover bids and information provided in connection with mergers.

B. The Financial Instruments Trading Act

56. Chapter 2 of the Financial Instruments Trading Act contains rules on prospectuses. A prospectus shall be prepared when financial instruments are offered to the public or are bought and sold on a regulated market unless the Act states that an exception is allowed. Such exceptions concern, for example, offers to qualified investors, to a limited number of investors or to investors that must make high minimum investments.

The idea is that a prospectus shall contain all the information that is needed in order to make a well-founded judgment on the issuer's result, status and foreseeable future. For further rules, the Act refers to Commission Regulation (EC) Number. 809/2004 implementing Directive 2003/71/EC of the European Parliament and of the European Council with regard to information contained in prospectuses as well as the format, incorporation by reference and publication of such prospectuses and dissemination of advertisements (text with EEA relevance) as well as to Regulation (EC) Number. 1060/2009 on credit rating agencies.

As to the form and content of a prospectus, the Act accepts it as drawn up as one document or as three separate documents: a registration document with information concerning the issuer, a securities document with information concerning the securities and a summary. If certain information is missing at the time when the prospectus is prepared, such information may be left out for the time being. However, the Financial Supervisory Authority shall be informed when the information is available. The information shall at the same time be made public.

The language in a prospectus issued in Sweden is usually Swedish. However, if a prospectus has been approved in another state within the EEA, only a summary in Swedish might be necessary.

It is the duty of the Financial Supervisory Authority to see to it that a prospectus is a complete document that is possible to understand in its different, connected parts, and also that the requirements of the Act and the above-mentioned regulation have been observed. It must be made public as soon as possible.

57. Chapter 2a of the Financial Instruments Trading Act (as amended in 2006) contains rules on prospectuses in connection with public takeover bids. As to the rules on takeovers, see paragraph 135 *infra*.

58. Chapter 4 of the Financial Instruments Trading Act contains rules on the obligations of a shareholder to disclose his/her number of shares when certain threshold values are passed.

IV. Distribution of Assets

A. *Background and Accounting Rules*

59. Chapter 17 of the Companies Act states in section 2 that value transfers from a company may take place only pursuant to the provisions in the Act regarding (1) distribution of profits, (2) acquisition of a company's own shares, (3) reduction of the share capital or statutory reserve for repayment to the shareholders and (4) certain kinds of gifts. The Act further states in Chapter 17, sections 3 and 4, the general conditions under which value transfers are permitted. These sections must be read together with Chapter 17, section 5, concerning gifts; Chapter 18, concerning distribution of profits (paragraph 71 *infra*); Chapter 19, concerning acquisition of the company's own shares (paragraphs 84 et seq. *infra*); and Chapter 20, concerning reductions of the share capital and the statutory reserve (paragraph 77 et seq. *infra*).

Disguised dividends are, although not mentioned in the Act, covered by what the Act states on permitted value transfers. Also covered there is any business event that has as a consequence the reduction of the company's assets and that is not of a purely commercial nature for the company (Chapter 17, section 1).

It may be added that a company's assets leave a company when it is merged with another company, when the company is de-merged and also when the company is wound up, but these situations are regulated separately and are not covered by the sections that concern value transfers.

It should be noted that when the Act speaks of distribution to the shareholders, it refers to distribution as such; shareholders may very well be third parties in relation to the company, and if they have sold something to the company, they are normal third parties (as long as they have not received special privileges because they are shareholders).

60. As already mentioned, the equity of a company is divided into two categories, restricted and non-restricted. Restricted equity is characterized by the fact that dividends and other payments to the shareholders as such are forbidden unless the restricted equity is left intact, while non-restricted equity is in principle free for distribution. This rule, of course, makes it necessary to decide both which equity is restricted – that is, should be preserved for the benefit of the creditors of the company and other third parties – and how the restriction manifests itself.

First, restricted equity is made up of the share capital, the revaluation reserve, the statutory (legal) reserve and the equity method reserve. The articles of association may – but very seldom do – add rules on restricted reserves. The share capital is created through the payments made by founders when the company was formed or in accordance with a resolution to increase the capital, through an accounting transaction in connection with a bonus issue, through the conversion of a convertible instrument or through payments according to conditions of warrants (see paragraphs 136–151 *infra*). The revaluation reserve is an alternative to revaluation of a fixed asset with a reliable and permanent value materially exceeding its previous balance sheet value, combined with an increase in the share capital (see Annual Reports Act, Chapter 4, section 6). The statutory (legal) reserve was earlier created through mandatory allocations of 10% of the net profit for each year, but the 2005 Companies Act does not contain any provision on transfers to a statutory (legal) reserve.

Second, the share capital and the two reserves just described are in reality nothing more than bookkeeping entries – the capital that the share capital and the reserves correspond to is used in the activities of the company. Fixed and current assets are bought with this capital. Consequently, the restriction finds expression in the balance sheet of the company.

61. The articles of association are required – among other things – to state the financial year of the company. The Companies Act states in turn (Chapter 7, sections 10 and 11) that an annual general meeting of shareholders must be held within six months of the end of each financial year and that the annual report and (unless the Company does not have an auditor, see IV *infra*) the audit report – and often, when the company is a parent company, also the consolidated report and the audit report on the group – are to be presented by the board at that meeting. The annual report in turn consists of an income statement, a balance sheet, notes and a directors' report. Sometimes a cash flow analysis must also be added to the annual report.

62. The annual report, including the income statement, the balance sheet and the notes, must be prepared according to *generally accepted accounting principles.*

63. The provisions of the 1995 Annual Reports Act (as later amended) apply both to the income statement and to the balance sheet contained in the annual report. The 1999 Accounting Act applies to the accounts. These are not made public, but the annual report – which will become public – is based on what the accounts contain.

64. The Accounting Act states in Chapter 4 what the requirement to maintain accounting records implies and goes in Chapter 5 into the obligation to maintain a current recording of transactions together with a supporting vouchers ledger and also a general ledger.

65. The Annual Reports Act gives in Chapter 2 some general and basic rules for all annual reports. They must be made in such a way that they are lucid and made according to generally accepted accounting principles. They must further give a fair presentation of the position and the result of the company. A company shall normally be supposed to continue its activities in the future. The same principles for valuation, classification, and so on shall normally be used every year. If there are special reasons for a deviation from what is said in the last two sentences, this is allowed on condition both that the annual report is made in a lucid way and according to generally accepted accounting principles and that it gives a fair presentation of the position and the result of the company. Chapter 3 gives details on the balance sheet and the income statement.

The *income statement* has to show, in a summarized form, the total income and expenses of the business during the financial year.

The Annual Reports Act stipulates the format for the income statement, with some exceptions called for by the nature and extent of the business.

The *balance sheet* has to show, in a summarized form, the total assets, provisions, liabilities and equity of the business at the balance sheet date. Pledged assets and contingent liabilities are to be shown as separate memorandum items.

The Annual Reports Act also stipulates the format for the balance sheet, with some exceptions called for by the nature and extent of the business.

However, small-sized companies are allowed to make one entry in the income statement and the balance sheet for certain items specified in the Act.

Additional – extensive – information on numerous topics must be given in the *notes*. This information concerns, for example, valuation and translation principles, different questions concerning fixed assets, tax assessment values, financial instruments, revaluation reserves, net sales in different branches and the total amount of salaries and other remuneration paid in large-sized and public companies during the financial year to (a) the board of directors and the managing director and (b) other employees. Bonus payments and similar remuneration to the board of directors and the managing director are to be stated separately. The notes shall also state the average number of employees, including a breakdown thereof between women and men.

All but small-sized companies must, under in the Act stated conditions, report on economic arrangements that are not shown in the balance sheet, if such information is necessary in order to obtain a fair presentation of the position of the company. And large-sized companies must also report on substantial transactions on not strict business lines vis-à-vis persons which are closely associated with the company. Such a duty has also any public company under in the Act stated conditions.

The *directors' report* shall contain information on numerous circumstances that are of importance for the assessment of the results and the financial position of the company. Significant events that have occurred during or since the end of the financial year are also to be reported here. The directors' report must also contain information on different topics concerning the number and quota values of the company's own shares – including those owned, bought and sold by the company – as well as the reasons for the company's acquisitions and transfers during the last financial year. For companies with shares on a regulated market, the demand for information goes much further than it does in other companies. The directors' report must also contain a proposal concerning the appropriation of the profit or loss of the company.

In all public companies with their securities on a regulated market, the directors' report must contain a corporate governance statement unless such a statement is made in the form of a separate document.

Large-sized companies must finally attach a *cash flow analysis* (*finansieringsanalys*) to their annual reports. This statement provides information on the company's sources of finance and capital investments during the financial year.

66. The Annual Reports Act often requires a parent company to prepare and make public, in addition to its own annual report, consolidated accounts consisting of a consolidated income statement, a consolidated balance sheet, notes, a directors' report and also a cash flow analysis. These accounts are to be prepared as of the same date as the parent company's balance sheet. See further paragraph 268 *infra*.

67. According to the Annual Reports Act, Chapter 9, some companies (credit institutions, securities companies and insurance companies) are obliged to submit an interim report containing information on the company's activities from the beginning of the financial year.

B. Examination of the Annual Report

68. After this broad survey of the annual report and the principles for its preparation, it is time to call attention to the fact that in all public and large-sized private companies someone has to examine both the accounts and the annual report – and in Sweden also the manner in which the board of directors and the managing director have administered the company – to make sure that it is all done and taken care of according to the law, including generally accepted accounting principles (the Companies Act, Chapter 9, section 3). This is the duty of the auditor or auditors of the company. The Annual Reports Act, Chapter 8, section 2, states that the annual report is to be handed over to them not less than six weeks before the annual general meeting of the shareholders. I will come back to the appointment of the auditors and their powers and duties later (paragraph 215 et seq. *infra*).

69. At the annual meeting of shareholders, which is to be held within six months of the end of each financial year, the annual report and the auditor's report are presented (Companies Act, Chapter 7, sections 10 and 11). At this meeting, resolutions are to be passed with respect to, among other items, adoption of the income statement and the balance sheet (and, where the company is a parent company that is obliged to prepare a group account, adoption of the consolidated income statement and consolidated balance sheet), appropriation of the company's profit or loss according to the adopted balance sheet and discharge of liability of the directors and the managing director. For companies whose shares are traded on a regulated market in Sweden, the annual general meeting shall also adopt resolutions regarding guidelines for compensation to senior management (the Companies Act, Chapter 8, section 23a).

Consideration of the resolutions concerning adoption of the income statement and the balance sheet, appropriation of the company's profit or loss, and discharge of liability must, however, be postponed until the general meeting is resumed at a later time if either a simple majority or a minority consisting of the owners of one-tenth of all shares so requests. This right of not only the majority but also a minority of shareholders is mandatory and affords the shareholders an opportunity to examine the material presented in greater depth than might have been possible during the period before the meeting when they had access to the income statement, the balance sheet, the notes, the directors' report and the auditor's report. It also creates the opportunity for negotiations. The general meeting must be resumed not earlier than four weeks and not later than eight weeks after the first meeting. Further adjournments are not permitted (Companies Act, Chapter 7, section 14).

70. Not later than one month after the income statement and balance sheet have been adopted, copies of the annual report (and the corporate governance statement if such a statement is made in the form of a separate document and has not been made public at the website of the company) and, if the company has an auditor, the auditor's report must be sent to the Companies Registration Office (Annual Reports Act, Chapter 8, section 3). A director or the managing director has to certify on the copy of the annual report that the income statement and the balance sheet have been adopted, giving the date of adoption. This certificate must also include details of the general meeting's resolution regarding the appropriation of the company's profit or loss (see paragraph 71 *infra*).

If copies of the annual report and the auditor's report have not been submitted in the prescribed manner within fifteen months of the end of the financial year, the directors and the managing director become jointly and severally liable for obligations that the company incurs unless a director or the managing director can prove that the failure to send in the annual report and the auditor's report was not caused by negligence on his/her part. Liability with respect to obligations incurred by the company does not arise after receipt of the documents by the Companies Registration Office (the 1995 Annual Reports Act, Chapter 8, section 12).

A company that does not submit certified copies of the annual report and the auditor's report in due time (normally within seven months of the end of the financial year) is normally liable to pay a special fee (which will be re-imposed after some time) (Annual Reports Act, Chapter 8, sections 5–11).

C. Dividends and Similar Forms of Distribution

71. The adoption of the balance sheet is important because it fixes the status of the balance sheet as of the balance sheet date; that is, the last day of the financial year. The maximum that may be used for dividends and other value transfers to the shareholders is what is stated in the balance sheet as the company's non-restricted equity. 'A value transfer may not take place where, after the transfer, there is insufficient coverage for the company's restricted equity', provided that 'the calculation shall be based on the most recently adopted balance sheet taking into consideration changes in restricted shareholders' equity which have occurred subsequent to the balance sheet date' and further, notwithstanding these conditions:

> that the company (or the group) may effect a value transfer to shareholders or another party only provided such appears to be justified taking into consideration both the demands with respect to the size of shareholders' equity which are imposed by the nature, scope and risk associated with the operations; and the company's (or the group's) need to strengthen its balance sheet, liquidity and financial position in general' (Companies Act, Chapter 17, section 3).

This last condition is referred to as the *prudence rule* of the Companies Act. (Incidentally, Chapter 20 of the Companies Act, on reduction of the share capital, also includes a prohibition on the payment of dividends; see paragraph 89 *infra*.)

Where the general meeting is to consider the matter of a distribution of profits, the board of directors shall prepare a proposed resolution pursuant to sections 3–6 in Chapter 18 of the Companies Act. One of these sections, Chapter 18, section 4, states that the board must state whether the proposed distribution of profits is justifiable in light of the prudence rule.

The decision concerning the distribution is made by a simple majority of those at the general meeting, but the meeting may not decide on a higher dividend than the board has proposed or accepted unless the owners of not less than one-tenth of all shares request distribution of profits according to the minority protection rule in Chapter 18, section 11, or a right to distribution has been included in the company's articles of association.

72. If a shareholder has received profits in violation of the provisions discussed in paragraph 71 *supra*, the recipient shall return what he/she has received where the company can prove that he/she knew or should have realized that the distribution was in violation of the Companies Act. If the shareholder was in bad faith, he/she will have to repay what he/she has received. This rule protects shareholders in good faith (Chapter 17, section 6).

Where a shareholder is not required to or cannot pay back what he/she has received, those who participated in the decision regarding the value transfer are liable in damages for the deficiency if they have shown intent or negligence (shareholders, however, are liable only if they have shown intent or gross negligence). Where a deficiency arises in connection with restitution pursuant to what has been set out here, any person who has received property from someone who was an unlawful recipient may be held liable if he/she knew that the property that he/she got was received in violation of the aforesaid provisions. See Chapter 17, section 7, paragraph 3.

73. What has been said so far concerns unlawful distribution of profits, but the rule is same both for reduction of the share capital or the statutory reserve for repayment to the shareholders and for gifts for charitable purposes. However, concerning business transactions that are not of a 100% commercial character, the company has an even stronger case when it comes to demand return of the unlawful 'gift', as the company only has to prove that the other party understood – or should have understood – that the transaction included a value transfer from the company: In other words, in these cases the transferee does not need to know that the Companies Act has been violated.

These rules concern mainly the protection of the creditors of companies. But there might be a need to protect the shareholders even if there is no danger for the creditors. It is thus possible to invoke the general clauses of the Companies Act – see paragraph 48 *supra* – in connection with actions for damages against disloyal board members or managing directors and maybe even against shareholders.

74. Although a company limited by shares has as its purpose the making of profits for its shareholders unless the articles of association provide otherwise, the Companies Act contains (in Chapter 17, section 5) a provision stating that gifts may be made for purposes of public benefit or for other purposes of a similar nature. This possibility is, however, dependent on – apart from the purpose – the gift being reasonable in view of its purpose, seen in relation to the financial position of the company and other relevant circumstances, if decided on by the general meeting, and on the gift being of minor importance with regard to the same factors if decided on by the board of directors.

D. Prohibition against Loans

75. A rule of great importance for the protection of a company's capital is the prohibition on a company granting cash loans or furnishing securities in certain situations. These rules are found in Chapter 21 of the Companies Act and can be seen as the necessary consequence of the rule that a company limited by shares cannot be registered – and thus constitute a legal person – unless the amount to be paid in cash for the shares has been paid to an account opened by the founders for such purpose and all property other than cash has been transferred to the company (paragraph 27 *supra*). This requirement would not mean very much if the shareholders – or the shareholder in a one-man company – could borrow from the company the money that they were required to pay in connection with its formation.

The prohibition begins in Chapter 21, section 1, with the rule that a company may not grant cash loans to (or furnish securities for) a person who owns shares in or who is a director or managing director of the company or of another company in the same group. Cash loans and securities are also prohibited if they are made to or furnished for close relatives of shareholders, directors and managing directors – viz. any person who is married to, or co-habits with, or is a sibling of or a relative in direct ascending or descending relationship to shareholders, directors and managing directors; or any person who is related by marriage to a shareholder, director or managing director in direct ascending or descending relationship or where either person is married to a sibling of the other; or a legal person in which any of the aforementioned persons, alone or together with any other person referred to in the enumeration, has a controlling influence.

These natural and legal persons could be referred to as *the prohibited group*.

There are, however, certain exceptions from the prohibition (Chapter 21, section 2). In summary, the provisions are not to apply where (1) the debtor is a municipality (*kommun*) or a county council (*landsting* or *kommunalförbund*); (2) the debtor is a legal person within the same group as the lending company; (3) the debtor operates a business, and the loan is given for purely business reasons; and (4) the loan has been taken by the Swedish National Debt Office pursuant to the State Borrowing and Debt Management Act.

There is also an exception concerning small shareholders. The prohibition does not apply to a shareholder or connected persons where the total number of company shares held by the borrower and connected persons does not amount to 1% of the share capital.

Quite apart from the general prohibition on loans and securities, Chapter 21, section 5, states that a company may not grant an advance or a cash loan or furnish a security for the purpose of financing the acquisition of its shares or shares in a parent company in the same group by the debtor or any related natural or legal person in the prohibited group.

However, the prohibition against loans and security for the purpose of financing the acquisition of shares in the lending or furnishing company or in another company in the same group is not applicable in some situations where the aim is general share ownership among the employees of a company and the advance, loan or security does not exceed two times the price base amount pursuant to the National Insurance Act (approximately somewhat less than SEK 90,000). This rule is intended to make it easier for employees to acquire shares in their employing (or a connected) company (Chapter 21, section 6). Such advances, loans or securities may not be granted, however, if their total amount would exceed the non-restricted equity of the company and the advance, loan or security would not be justifiable in light of the prudence rule.

76. These rules will, of course, hinder the transfer of companies to natural and legal persons other than those with assets of their own. This could mean the destruction in the long run of all or most small companies in Sweden. The Companies Act therefore contains an exception to the prohibition on loans and securities that states that the Swedish Tax Office (*Skatteverket*) or, where relevant, the Financial Supervisory Authority may, upon application, grant permission to provide an advance, loan or security for the acquisition of shares in the company or another company in the group if this is justified by special circumstances (Chapter 21, section 8). Exemptions pursuant to this rule may, however, not be granted with respect to the acquisition of shares in a public company through an advance, loan or security (Chapter 21, section 12).

E. Reduction of the Share Capital

77. We now come to reductions in the share capital and the statutory reserve. The rules on such reductions are found in Chapter 20 of the Companies Act.

78. It is normally the general meeting that decides to reduce the share capital when this capital has become larger than is deemed necessary. The articles of association might, however, provide that the share capital may be reduced by redemption of shares. The two alternatives will be described in turns, beginning with reductions in general. The rules on reduction due to a clause in the articles of associations will be discussed in paragraph 82 *infra*.

79. The share capital and the statutory reserve are entries in the balance sheet that are recorded as restricted equity. They reduce the free capital in the balance sheet – that is, what can be paid to the shareholders as profit – and thus fulfil the task of safeguarding the creditors. But if a company has had losses that cannot be covered by non-restricted equity, such losses will be reflected in a reduction in the restricted equity. First, the statutory reserve will be wiped out through a decision to this effect by the general meeting (see Chapter 20, sections 35 and 36), and then the share capital will be eroded. It should be mentioned in this connection that whenever there is reason to assume that the equity of the company is less than half of the registered share capital, the board of directors is obliged to take special action, at the risk of personal liability (see paragraph 88 et seq. *infra*).

80. A reduction of the share capital may take place for covering losses in the share capital where unrestricted shareholders' equity equal to the losses is not available, for transfer to a fund to be used pursuant to a resolution adopted by the general meeting or for direct repayment to the shareholders.

If the share capital has become larger than is deemed necessary, the general meeting may by a majority of at least two-thirds both of the votes and of the shares represented at the meeting – and on the condition that the board of directors agrees – decide that the share capital shall be reduced, provided, however, that the reduction is justifiable in light of the prudence rule and that the auditor of the company has submitted a written statement as to whether, according to his/her opinion, the general meeting should reduce the share capital. Also other conditions must be met. Such reduction can be carried out either with or without retirement of shares.

If the articles of association need to be amended, a resolution to that effect must also be made.

81. The resolution to reduce the share capital must in these two situations be recorded by the Companies Registration Office and may not be carried out until either the Companies Registration Office or the appropriate district court has checked that the reduction can take place without any risk to the creditors of the company.

82. As indicated above, reduction of the share capital may also take place pursuant to a clause in the articles of association. Such a reduction presupposes, however, according to the Companies Act, Chapter 20, section 31, that the articles specify a maximum and a minimum share capital; the capital may never be reduced below the minimum limit. The provision must also specify the order and amount of the redemption or the basis for its calculation. A reduction may normally not be carried out unless either the Companies Registration Office or an appropriate district court has checked that the reduction can take place without any danger to the creditors of the company. If, however, the restricted equity would be fully covered after the reduction and an amount of the same size as the reduction is transferred to the statutory reserve, such approval is not necessary.

The resolution to reduce the share capital may, if the articles of association so provide, be a task for the board. Otherwise, the decision is in this situation adopted by the general meeting of shareholders with only a simple majority (Chapter 20, section 32).

The resolution to reduce the share capital must be recorded by the Companies Registration Office.

F. Reduction of the Statutory Reserve

83. Also the statutory reserve may be reduced. Such reduction may, for example, take place in connection with a bonus or a new issue. But a reduction may also take place for repayment to the shareholders. This last alternative is treated in the same way as repayment of the share capital to the shareholders.

G. Acquisition of the Company's Own Shares

84. After having discussed reductions of the share capital and the statutory reserve, we now come to the Companies Act, Chapter 19, on acquisition of the company's own shares.

A reduction of the share capital can also be effected by a company acquiring its own shares. Therefore, the Swedish Companies Act has long included the stipulations that a company was not allowed to subscribe for its own shares or to buy or receive as security its own shares. To avoid evasion of these rules, subsidiaries were also forbidden to subscribe for shares or to acquire or receive as security shares in the parent company. There were, however, some exceptions from the prohibition to buy shares or to receive shares as security. A company could, for example, acquire an enterprise that owned shares in the acquiring company. A company could, furthermore, acquire its own shares at a public auction when these shares had been seized to satisfy the claims of the company. And a company could also redeem its own shares when, in an action under the Companies Act, a court had ordered it to do so (see paragraph 235 *infra*).

The shares that the company acquired according to these exceptions were to be disposed of as soon as they could be sold without a loss and not later than three years after acquisition.

If a company became a parent company and the subsidiary owned shares in the parent, these shares were to be disposed of in the same way as when a company acquired an enterprise that owned shares in the acquiring company.

These rules are now contained in Chapter 19, sections 1 et seq.

85. The rules on acquisition of the company's own shares were, however, amended in 2000 to give public companies with listed shares a limited right to acquire and transfer their own shares. These rules were in the 2005 Companies Act transferred to Chapter 19, sections 13 et seq. They allow, under conditions specified in the Act, public companies the right to acquire their own shares on a regulated market or, following authorization by the Swedish Financial Supervisory Authority, an equivalent regulated market outside the EEA or in accordance with an offer that has been directed to all shareholders or all holders of a special class of shares. An acquisition of the company's own shares may, however, not be carried out if it could endanger the protection of the restricted equity of the company or could come in conflict with the prudence rule. Neither may a company acquire its own shares to the extent that the company's holding of its own shares would exceed one-tenth of all shares in the company (Chapter 9, section 15). If a company has acquired its own shares in conflict with what the Act states, the shares must be disposed of within six months or the shares may be declared void (Chapter 19, section 16).

Resolutions concerning the acquisition of a company's own shares are to be adopted by the general meeting or, after the authorization of the general meeting, by the board of directors (Chapter 19, section 17). Such resolutions are valid only where they are supported by shareholders holding not less than two-thirds of both the votes cast and the shares represented at the general meeting.

86. The Companies Act also contains rules on acquisition and transfer of the company's own warrants and convertible instruments (Chapter 19, sections 10–12). According to these rules, an acquisition of warrants and convertible instruments is allowed on the condition that it does not endanger the protection of the restricted equity of the company and does not come in conflict with the prudence rule. The company can transfer warrants, but not convertible instruments that it has acquired.

H. Repayment in Connection with the Winding-Up of the Company

87. A company's assets may be distributed to the shareholders not only in the form of dividends, in connection with a reduction in the share capital or the statutory reserve and through the acquisition of the company's own shares, but also in connection with the winding-up of the company. Repayment when the company no longer needs any capital is natural and somewhat different from the other situations. The last one of these situations will be discussed later, see paragraphs 238 et seq. *infra*.

V. Deficiency in the Share Capital

88. Whenever there is reason to assume that the equity of the company is less than half of the registered share capital, the board of directors is under an obligation to take special action. This rule is based on the knowledge that it is impossible (whatever rules the legislature might prescribe) to prevent a company from losing its assets – what the legislature can do is to try to put a stop to activities that are dangerous to creditors and other third parties (including individual shareholders). Rules to this end are found in Chapter 25, sections 13–20, of the Companies Act. Section 13 begins by stating that (1) whenever there is reason to assume that the equity of the company is less than half of the registered share capital or (2) whenever the company, in connection with a seizure pursuant to Chapter 4 of the Debt Recovery Code, has been found to lack sufficient seizable assets for full payment of the debt, the board of directors must without delay prepare a special balance sheet and have the auditor (if there is any) examine it. If the balance sheet shows that more than half of the share capital has been lost, there is a great risk that the company will soon be in bankruptcy.

Therefore, the board is under an obligation to submit to a general meeting, as soon as possible, the choice between an immediate winding-up and a reconstruction of the company. If, on the other hand, the balance sheet shows that half or more of the share capital is covered by the equity of the company, its activities may go on as before without any requirement to take special action – until, perhaps, there is once again reason to assume that the equity is less than half the registered share capital or a new unsuccessful seizure has taken place.

When the board has called a general meeting and this meeting decides that the company is to be wound up, a liquidation process starts. We will come back to this later (paragraphs 238 et seq. *infra*). But if the general meeting wishes the company to continue its activities and votes accordingly (by a simple majority), it is the task of the board of directors to do what it can to get the company reconstructed. One alternative might be that the business activities of the company are so successful that its net profits will fill the gaps in its equity. This, however, is not what is meant by reconstruction. For a true, 100% reconstruction, there are different alternatives.

89. The first of these is to reduce the share capital by at least the amount that is missing. A reduction in this situation does not involve money being repaid to the shareholders, and there is no need for the approval of the court at this stage of the procedure, as is the case when a reduction is combined with repayment to the shareholders. But the resolution has to be adopted by the general meeting of shareholders with a qualified majority – it is valid only where supported by shareholders holding not less than two-thirds of the votes cast and shares represented at the meeting. Where the company has several classes of shares, a qualified majority is needed in each class of shares represented at the meeting whose rights are prejudiced by the resolution (Chapter 20, section 5). The resolution must, according to Chapter 20, section 7, specify the purpose of the reduction; the amount or the maximum amount or the minimum and maximum amounts by which the share capital is to be reduced; whether the reduction is to be effected with or without retirement of shares and, where applicable, the shares that are to be retired. The resolution to reduce the share capital has to be registered in the Companies Register within four months of the resolution (Chapter 20, section 19). The reduction takes effect when the resolution is registered. Within a period of three years from the date of registration, however, dividends may in this situation normally be declared only if the Companies Registration Office or, in disputed cases, the appropriate district court so permits or the share capital has been increased by an amount corresponding at least to the amount of the reduction (see Chapter 20, section 30). Permission will in disputed cases be granted by the court only if the creditors of the company have been consulted and either do not object or receive payment or satisfactory security for their claims.

90. The second reconstruction alternative is to offer a new issue at a premium, which, as a minimum, allows the gap in the registered share capital to be filled. A new issue where the company receives only the quota value of the new shares will not wipe out any gap. The assets of the company will increase in value, but so, too, will the share capital – on the other 'side' of the balance sheet, under the heading of equity and liabilities. The gap will remain, but at a higher level. However, if payment for the shares includes an extra amount, this amount will improve the ratio of the assets of the company to the share capital.

91. The third alternative is to donate the missing amount to the company; gifts will increase the value of the assets without any allocation on the other 'side' of the balance sheet. It should be added that this alternative is in reality possible only in companies with a limited number of shareholders, since few shareholders would be willing to supply the company with assets of any kind without compensation – gifts to the company are usually based on some kind of agreement between the shareholders concerning compensation in the future. But it is essential that the company has no obligation to pay back the sums contributed. If repayment were expected, there would be no gift, and there would be a liability to enter in the balance sheet – and there would still be the same gap.

92. The time that the board of directors and the managing director have at their disposal to reconstruct the company is eight months. Unless, Chapter 25, section 16, of the Companies Act states, a general meeting of shareholders within eight months from the submission approves a balance sheet, examined by the auditor (if there is any), showing that as of the date of the shareholders' meeting the equity of the company amounts to the registered share capital – that is, unless the shortfall in the share capital is totally wiped out – the company has to be wound up. This means that if the reconstruction has succeeded, the general meeting can decide that the company is to go on with its activities without further problems (until, for example, there is once again reason to assume that the equity of the company is less than half the registered share capital, at which point the process starts all over again). But if the equity of the company is still less than the registered share capital, the general meeting is supposed to vote (by a simple majority; see Companies Act, Chapter 25, section 2) for the liquidation of the company. If it does not, the board of directors must – according to the Act, Chapter 25, section 17 – apply to the appropriate district court for an order for the winding-up of the company. Such an application may also be made by any director, the managing director, an auditor or any shareholder. Where such an application is made, the court orders the company to be wound up unless it is proven during the court proceedings that a balance sheet showing that the equity of the company amounts to the registered share capital and approved by a general meeting of shareholders. If the company has an appointed auditor, the balance sheet must be examined by him/her before it can be approved by the general meeting.

93. The 1995 Annual Reports Act sets out the values at which different assets may be stated in the annual accounts. The valuation principles are on the whole based on a concept of prudence. It is therefore quite possible that these principles will prove destructive in connection with the balance sheets that are to be prepared both whenever there is reason to believe that too much equity has been lost and for the second general meeting following reconstruction. To avoid forcing the liquidation of a company with a better status than would follow from the general accounting principles (e.g., with hidden reserves), the Companies Act (Chapter 25, section 14) provides additional rules for calculating the amount of the company shareholders' equity. The section states, first, that assets may be reported at a higher value and liabilities may be reported at a lower value than in the ordinary accounting, provided the valuation principles used in the preparation of the balance sheet for liquidation purposes are consistent with generally accepted accounting principles. Pension commitments, which pursuant to section 8a of the 1967 Pension Commitments (Security) Act have been entered as a sub-item under the heading 'Provisions for pensions and similar obligations', may, however, not be reported at a lower amount than is permissible pursuant to section 7 of the same Act. Second, assets may be reported at net realizable values. Third, liabilities resulting from government aid where the restitution obligation is dependent on the company's financial position need not be reported if, in the event of bankruptcy or liquidation, such aid is to be repaid only after other liabilities have been paid. In the second paragraph of the section, it is stated that untaxed reserves shall be allocated between shareholders' equity and deferred tax liability.

94. The board of directors is thus obliged to prepare a balance sheet whenever there is reason to assume that the equity of the company is less than half of the registered share capital or when the company is found to lack seizable assets, to call a general meeting if this balance sheet shows that the equity of the company is less than half of the registered share capital, to call a second general meeting if the company has not gone into liquidation in connection with the first general meeting and to apply to the appropriate district court for an order for the winding-up of the company if the new balance sheet does not show that the equity of the company amounts to the registered share capital. All these obligations need some kind of sanction if they are to be effective. And this sanction is the joint and several liability of the individual directors for the obligations of the company incurred from the time that the action should have been taken. But other persons can also become jointly and severally liable together with the directors if they act on behalf of the company and are aware of what the directors have neglected to do. The persons who can incur such liability are normally only the managing director and top executives. The personal liability that would otherwise rest on directors can, however, be avoided if a director proves that his/her failure to act was not caused by negligence. This general rule was added to the Companies Act instead of a rule making trade union (employee) representatives on the board automatically free from all personal liability.

95. From the time of the second general meeting, however, ordinary shareholders can also become personally liable for the debts of the company. This is a penalty for taking part in a decision at the second general meeting to go on with the activities of the company in spite of the fact that the company should, under Chapter 25, section 17, be wound up. However, directors, the managing director, top executives and individual shareholders are not liable with respect to obligations that have been incurred after the question of winding-up the company has been referred to the court for consideration; after a balance sheet showing that the equity amounts to the registered share capital has been examined by the auditor (if there is any) and approved by the general meeting; *or* after the general meeting, the Companies Registration Office *or* a court has resolved to pursue liquidation or issued a liquidation order.

VI. Classes of Shares

96. Chapter 4 of the Companies Act, which deals with shares, states in section 1 that all shares carry equal rights in the company unless otherwise provided in sections 2–5 of that same chapter. The only exceptions that are allowed are thus those that can be found in these sections. Section 2 states that an exception from the rule of equal rights can be made through provisions in the articles of association that state that shares of different classes shall, or may, be issued. These classes very often entail different economic rights – that is, different rights to share in the profits, to participate in increases in the share capital through new issues, and so on. Shares that give their holders preferential rights to the assets and profits of the company are usually referred to as preference shares (*preferensaktier*) and the others as ordinary shares (*stamaktier*). But the difference between the classes is not necessarily economic. A common difference is that some classes of shares carry a greater number of votes than other classes. These are not the only possible differences, however. Owners of a special class of shares might have the right to elect a certain number of directors and/or auditors. The differences between different classes of shares may also be of both an economic and some other nature. Very often preference shares carry fewer votes than ordinary shares.

One line, however, must never be crossed: Shares without basic membership rights are not permitted in Sweden. Companies are thus not allowed to issue a class of shares, the owners of which may not attend the general meeting of shareholders or vote at such meetings or take legal action against the company for an amendment or annulment of a resolution of the general meeting. The opinion of the Swedish legislature has been that it should not be possible to deprive a shareholder as an owner of a fraction of the company, however small, of the most basic elements of ownership.

The reasoning behind the prohibition against issuing shares without any votes also led the Swedish legislature in the 1975 Companies Act to outlaw the issuance of debentures that were to be repaid in relation to the dividends, their share in the property of the company or the market value of the shares at the time of repayment of the loan or of liquidation of the company. Such repayment conditions would, it was thought, in fact mean that the position of the holders of debentures would be more or less the same as that of shareholders – but without any votes. But the legislature changed its position in the 2005 Companies Act. The prohibition against this kind of debentures has ceased (the Companies Act, Chapter 11, section 11). The parties to a loan agreement have to weigh the different risks that may be at stake against the profit that they may realize from the agreement.

97. If the articles of association provide that the company shall have or may issue different classes of shares, the articles must, according to the Companies Act, Chapter 4, section 2, specify (1) the differences between the classes of shares and (2) the number of shares in each class. Where a provision pursuant to section 2 states that the shares shall carry different rights to the company's assets or profits or that the shares shall carry different voting rights, the provision shall state the pre-emption rights that vest in the shareholders in conjunction with any new issue of shares or warrants or convertible instruments when payment does not take the form of non-cash consideration (Chapter 4, section 3). This section continues by stating in some detail what a provision regarding pre-emption shall entail. According to section 4, where a provision states that the shares in the company shall not carry equal rights in the company's assets or profits, the articles of association shall also state the right to new shares that vests in the shareholders in the event of an increase in the share capital through a bonus issue.

98. These provisions concerning different classes of shares and pre-emption rights are referred to in the beginning of the four chapters of the Companies Act that deal with increases in share capital – that is, Chapter 12 on bonus issues and Chapter 13 on new issues, as well as Chapter 14 on issues of warrants and Chapter 15 on issues of convertible instruments.

Chapter 12 refers in section 2, paragraph 2, to the situation when a company has issued classes of shares that differ in relation to the entitlement to share in the company's assets or profits; in such a situation, the shareholder shall be entitled to receive new shares in accordance with the provisions of the articles of association pursuant to Chapter 4, section 4. When, on the other hand, a company has issued classes of shares that do not differ in entitlement to assets or profits, new shares shall be issued pro rata to the number of shares of the same class that are already in existence. In conjunction therewith, the old shares shall carry an entitlement to new shares of the same class pro rata to their portion of the share capital.

Chapter 13 states in section 1, paragraph 1, that in conjunction with new issues pursuant to that chapter, the shareholders shall, as a rule, hold pre-emption rights to the number of shares they own. But paragraph 2 states that the provision of paragraph 1 shall not apply where (1) the shares are to be paid for with non-cash consideration or (2) the pre-emption rights are to be governed in another manner as a consequence of such provisions of the articles of association as referred to in Chapter 4, section 3. Paragraph 2 continues by stating that paragraph 1 also shall not apply where the pre-emption rights are to be governed according to terms and conditions that have been issued in conjunction with an earlier issue of warrants or an earlier issue of convertible instruments *or* where provisions of the issue resolution stipulate otherwise.

The provisions of these regulations are also applicable to issues of warrants in Chapter 14 and convertible instruments in Chapter 15 *mutatis mutandis*; see Chapter 14, section 1, and Chapter 15, section 1.

99. Chapter 4, section 5, provides that where the difference between classes of shares relates to voting rights, no share may have a voting right exceeding ten times the voting right of any other share. This is a mandatory rule first introduced in the Companies Act of 1944, which preceded the 1975 and 2005 acts. Not exceeding means that a voting difference of less than a factor of ten is permissible. The difference between the number of votes carried by a share and its quota value (the share of the share capital) has both now and then led the legislature to prescribe that not only the number of votes, but also the number of shares is to be taken into account in different voting situations – for example, with regard to amendments to the articles of association. This rule on voting differences in the Companies Act is in fact a compromise between, on the one side, the wish to adhere to the principle that the size of an investment and the power that follows from it should correspond and, on the other side, the desire to facilitate stable management, company formation and reconstruction. The question of whether Sweden should abandon this possibility of voting differences and adhere to the principle of one-share-one-vote has been very much debated. The need for strong company leaders, however, is an argument in favour of these differences being retained.

Larger voting differences than one to ten can still be found in companies founded before the 1944 Act came into force. The new, mandatory rule has not been made retroactive.

100. It is permissible to prescribe in the articles of association that a shareholder shall have one vote for every fifth share that he/she owns, but not that a shareholder needs five shares to receive one vote. In the first case, the shareholder may vote when he/she has only one share, but he/she will not get two votes until he/she has six; in the second case, he/she would be without a vote until he/she had the prescribed minimum number of shares. The articles of association may also stipulate that shares of one class carry more votes than those of another class on questions of a special kind. But voting differences may not be connected to the shares being owned by a certain person.

101. Chapter 4, section 6, contains the rule that the articles of association may provide that shares of a certain class may be converted into shares of another class. If the articles contain such a rule, they must also state the conditions under which the conversion is to take place and if the conversion is to be initiated by the company or by the shareowner. The possibility of issuing convertible shares has been given to companies as, for example, a way of attracting capital when the market is probably not willing to subscribe for new shares unless it is given the extra security that preferential shares offer, but still demands the extra 'bonus' that subsequent conversion into an ordinary class of shares would mean.

Conversion shall be notified for registration without delay.

102. One difference that was still found in Sweden in 1992 but that had nothing to do with differing classes of shares was the difference between shares that could only be owned by Swedes and Swedish legal persons (in reality legal persons controlled by a majority of Swedes and other 'non-dangerous' persons) and shares that could also be owned by non-Swedes and non-Swedish legal persons. This is a distinction, however, that disappeared after 1992.

VII. Right to Transfer Shares

103. Chapter 4, section 7, of the Companies Act states that shares may be freely transferred and acquired unless otherwise provided by sections 8, 18 and 27 of the same chapter or by law. The free transfer of shares is deemed to be one of the basic principles for the protection of shareholders, who can (usually) only make their investments available by selling their shares.

VIII. Restrictions in the Free Transfer of Shares and a Right of Pre-emption

104. Chapter 4, section 8, of the Companies Act states that the articles of association of a company that is not a CSD company may include a provision pursuant to which one or more shares may be transferred to a new owner only with the company's consent (*consent clause*). A consent clause shall state whether the general meeting or the board shall consider a request for consent, the types of transfers that require the company's consent, whether the company shall be entitled to grant or refuse consent with respect to a smaller number of shares than the number covered by the request for consent, the terms for acquisition by another transferee where so requested by the transferor, the period of time within which the company shall issue a decision on the issue of consent, the period of time within which proceedings regarding consent can be brought to a court or to arbitrators and the period of time within which payment shall be made for shares acquired by another transferee.

105. Chapter 4, section 18, of the Companies Act states that the articles of association of a company that is not a CSD company may include a clause pursuant to which a shareholder or other party shall be invited to purchase a share before it is transferred to a new owner (*right of first refusal clause*). Such a clause shall state the type of transfers covered by the clause, whether the right of first refusal offer may be exercised with respect to a smaller number of shares than the shares covered by the offer, the holders of first refusal rights and the order *inter se* in which they shall be invited to purchase or the manner in which rights of first refusal are allocated between them, terms governing a purchase pursuant to rights of first refusal, the period of time within which demands to exercise such rights of first refusal must be presented to the company, the period of time within which proceedings can be brought to a court or to arbitrators and the period of time within which payment must be made for shares purchased pursuant to rights of first refusal.

106. Chapter 4, section 27, of the Companies Act states that the articles of association may provide that shareholders or others shall have a right of post-transfer purchase where the title of a share has passed to a new owner (*post-transfer purchase right clause*). A provision on post-transfer purchase shall state the type of transfers covered by the clause, whether an offer regarding a post-transfer purchase right may be exercised with respect to a smaller number of shares than the shares covered by the offer, the holders of post-transfer purchase rights, terms governing the purchase, the period of time within which demands to exercise such purchase rights must be presented to the company, the period of time within which proceedings regarding post-transfer purchase rights can be brought to a court or to arbitrators and the period of time within which payment must be made for purchased shares.

Post-transfer purchase right clauses can also be used by CSD companies, but they are in fact only used by companies with a limited number of shareholders.

A person who has acquired shares covered by a post-transfer purchase right clause may not be entered into the share register until the question of pre-emption is resolved. Thus, he/she may not – unless the articles of association stipulate otherwise – use the votes connected with the shares until the dispute is over. This means in fact that the power over the company can be affected. But questions concerning dividends and other matters that cannot wait are covered by a section in the Act that states who shall represent the shares when they have no registered owner (see Chapter 4, section 35, of the Companies Act).

Finally, the Act on Public Takeover Bids on the Stock Market provides that the articles of association of certain companies may include the provision that a post-transfer purchase right clause shall in certain situations be without any effect. (On takeovers in general, see paragraph 135 *infra*.)

IX. Transfer of Shares

107. As for transfers of shares and the registration of shareholders, there are two different systems in Sweden: a traditional one still used by companies with a small or limited number of shareholders and a newer one designed for large companies. In companies that apply the latter system, there are neither share certificates nor coupons. Such companies are referred to as CSD companies (*avstämningsbolag*) (see paragraphs 118 et seq. *infra*).

108. Before we go any further, one point should be made. No company limited by shares can exist without shares. But the issuance of share certificates is voluntary unless such certificates are demanded by the shareholders in companies that still use the traditional system. Share certificates probably exist rather rarely in one-man companies. This should be borne in mind in relation to the discussion of share certificates below.

A. The Traditional System

109. The Companies Act sets out in Chapter 6, section 2, the information that share certificates must contain: the company's business name; the company registration number and company category; the shareholder's name, ID or registration number or other identification number; the number of shares to which the certificate relates; the classes of shares, where there may be different classes of shares pursuant to the articles of association; certain clauses in the articles of association of special importance to shareholders; and the date of issuance of the share certificate.

110. The share register (*aktieboken*) is a register in which all the shares and shareholders of the company are recorded (whether or not share certificates are issued). It may be an ordinary bound book, but a loose-leaf system or a computerized system is also possible.

111. The share register is of great importance. Share certificates may be delivered only to shareholders who are entered in this register. If later a share certificate is transferred to a new owner by a person who has it in his/her hand and can show its transfer in writing to him/her – in one or several stages – the transferee is deemed to be the proper owner and shall be registered in the share register. This presupposes, however, that, if the transferor lacked the right to perform the transfer, the new owner did not act imprudently. The transfer is usually endorsed on the share certificate as such. The name of a shareholder in the share register makes it unnecessary to prove transfers further back.

112. If a share certificate is transferred or pledged, the transferee is protected in relation to the creditors of the transferor or pledgor only if the transferee has the share certificate in his/her possession.

113. The share register is open for inspection by anyone (Chapter 5, section 10). This might be of importance to a shareholder who wishes to contact his/her fellow shareholders, but representatives of the public, such as journalists, may sometimes also be interested in the share register of a certain company. The basic element is the share, and this means that the names of the shareholders appear in the register in the order in which they purchased the different shares they own. Thus, it can take considerable time for a person inspecting the register to determine who owns what. This, of course, forces many companies to have other registers as well – for example, a register that shows each shareholder and the shares he/she owns. But on such registers, the Act is silent, and, consequently, such documents are not public. If the share register is computerized, the company is obliged to supply an enquirer with an update.

114. One of the main reasons the share register is important is the fact that the entry in that register of a person as a shareholder is a necessary precondition for his/her taking part in the activities of the company – with the exception of such rights as are connected to share coupons (if such coupons have been issued). This means that a shareholder who has not been registered cannot participate in a shareholders' meeting (at least not as a shareholder) and he/she cannot bring an action against the resolutions passed at such a meeting unless he/she has been improperly denied registration.

Not uncommonly, a person who saw his/her shares in a company as an investment and who had no interest in attending the meetings of the company and other similar activities would not register. His/her interest was in the dividend he/she might receive and in the increase in the value of his/her shares – for the first thing, coupons were used, and for the second, he/she needed no registration as a shareholder. This might, however, now be history to some extent, since the types of companies of interest to such investors are nowadays mostly CSD companies, and in these, you have to be registered if you are to derive any benefit from and enjoy the necessary protection for your shares.

115. It should be added, however, that in section 45 of Chapter 8 (on the management of the company), the Companies Act states that any director and managing director shall, when taking up his/her office, give notice of his/her holding of shares in the company and in companies in the same group unless such entry has already been made in the register. Changes in such shareholdings, furthermore, must be notified within one month. (These provisions are not applicable when there is already an obligation to notify under the Notification Obligation Act; see paragraph 131 *infra.*) This requirement is stated because of the information that the company as such needs concerning shares in the company or the group of companies held by the management. If, for example, the managing director sells most of the shares he/she owns in the company, the board of directors could very well have good reason to ask themselves – and the managing director – why he/she has sold them.

116. The Companies Act also includes provisions (Chapter 6, section 9) on interim certificates (*interimsbevis*), which may be used before any share certificate can be issued. Interim certificates can also be used in certain other situations. The number of new shares that a shareholder is entitled to subscribe for in connection with a new issue or a bonus issue is not always quite the same as the number of shares he/she already holds. He/she could, for example, have the right to subscribe for one new share for every five old ones. To give the shareholders an opportunity to sell or buy remaining partial certificates – that is, to give them an opportunity to get rid of or gather, in our example, 1–4 partial certificates – the Companies Act states in Chapter 11, section 4, that issue certificates (*emissionsbevis*) can be issued: fractional scrip certificates (*fondaktiebevis*) in connection with bonus issues and subscription right certificates (*teckningsrättsbevis*) in the case of new issues.

117. Coupons (*utdelningskuponger*) are common in the kinds of companies that still use share certificates. These coupons either have numbers or state the financial year they represent. A single coupon can be sold, but not the right to all future dividends, unless the share to which it is attached is sold at the same time. When a decision on the distribution of profits has been made, the coupon for the year is looked upon as a promissory note made out to the bearer – the coupon gives the bearer quite good protection. But before a decision on profit distribution is made, the bearer of the coupon as such is not protected by the rules of good faith.

Coupons fall under a special statute of limitations running three years from the date they could first be used. If someone informs the company within that time that a coupon has been destroyed or lost and the statement is shown to be plausible, he/she has the right to receive the payment that was earlier associated with the coupon without producing it (see the Promissory Notes Act, section 25).

B. The CSD System

118. The other system for the registration of shares, shareholders, and so on and for the transfer of shares is the CSD system (*avstämningsbolagssystemet*).

Provisions concerning this system are found in both the Companies Act and the Financial Instruments (Accounts) Act.

119. The CSD system is administered by different enterprises that have been authorized to act with shares and other instruments in the companies that are attached to this system.

120. No share certificates or other certificates may be used in companies connected to this system – these documents have been replaced by a computerized registration system, to which the banks and security brokers that have received approval are connected. The shares are thus registered in accounts that are opened for each shareholder with his/her securities company. When shares and other instruments are issued, sold or disposed of, a registration takes place in the account of the relevant shareholder.

121. The share register, containing largely the same information as the share registers of non-CSD companies, is also computerized. One additional possibility, and a possibility of great importance in the share registers of CSD companies, is that of entering the names of nominee shareholders in the share register (Companies Act, Chapter 5, section 14). In a CSD company, a nominee – for example, a bank or a securities institution – may thus be entered in the share register instead of the holder of the shares entrusted to the nominee.

122. The decision to transform a company into a CSD company is made by the general meeting adopting a resolution to include in the articles of association a provision to the effect that the person who, on a given record day (*avstämningsdag*), is recorded in the share register or the special register of shares shall, subject to restrictions (see paragraph 124 *infra*), be entitled to receive dividends and, at bonus issues, new shares and to exercise the shareholder's preferential right to participate in an issue of new shares. Companies whose articles contain such a provision, referred to as a record-day clause (*avstämningsförbehåll*), are in this book called CSD companies (in Chapter 1, section 10, *avstämningsbolag*).

123. The Financial Instruments (Accounts) Act states that every person who owns shares and other financial instruments that are registered according to the same Act must in principle have one or several control accounts. Such an account shall, *inter alia*, generally contain details of the account holder's name, identification number and postal address; the names, identification numbers and postal addresses of pledgees and others who have certain rights connected with a financial instrument; the number of financial instruments in the account; a statement as to whether the shares have been fully paid up; the class of shares to which the shares belong, if relevant; whether the shares are convertible, if relevant; pre-emption clauses relevant to the shares; payments that have diminished the quotient value of the shares, etc.; and the names and addresses of guardians, custodians, pledgees and other persons that are to receive dividends, etc., on behalf or instead of the shareholder, etc.

124. Since no share certificates or other documents are issued, all rights connected with a share go to the shareholder unless the shares are subject to restrictions. The registration makes it possible to direct the distribution of profits and bonus shares, as well as the right to participate in new issues, to the proper person, although the shareholder retains his/her right to appear as a shareholder at general meetings of the company.

125. In a system without share certificates and other documents, questions concerning ownership are answered on the basis of registration. The person – natural or artificial – who is registered as the shareholder is supposed to be the owner in relation both to the company and to third parties. If the same shares are sold twice, the one who is registered first will normally keep them. The same rule is applied in connection with pledging.

126. Why then this computerized system? There are two main reasons. The first of these has to do with the cost aspect – it is much cheaper to have a system without documents, where all transactions can be performed in a computerized system. And the second reason has to do with society's wish to be able to keep itself informed of major shareholdings and large shareholders. The share register, which – as have already been pointed out when commenting on the traditional system – is open for inspection by anyone, becomes extremely open in a computerized system. Such a system makes it possible to obtain the information you want extremely quickly and easily. This ready access to information has even made the legislature hesitate, and it is stated in the Companies Act that shareholders with 500 or fewer shares in a CSD company shall not be included in a transcript of the share register open to third parties unless there is only one shareholder with 500 or fewer shares (Chapter 5, section 19).

127. Any shareholder with a nominee who wishes to play an active part in the activities of the company must further register as a shareholder the day when the share register for the meeting is processed (see paragraph 154 *infra*). Regarding the general meeting, the Companies Act states in Chapter 7, section 28, that in companies that are not CSD companies, the entire share register showing the position at the day of the meeting must be kept available at the meeting, while in CSD companies, a transcript of the entire share register showing the position not more than five days before the meeting shall be kept available for inspection by the shareholders at that meeting.

X. Securities Market Legislation, Takeovers

128. Long before Sweden had to implement any European Council directive, the Swedish Industry and Commerce Stock Exchange Committee (the *Näringslivets börskommitté, NBK*) was formed by the Stockholm Chamber of Commerce and the Federation of Swedish Industries. The Committee was given the tasks of issuing recommendations to strengthen the stock market ethic and thus to further good behaviour in the market and of addressing important questions concerning the stock market. The Panel on Takeovers and Mergers in London served as a model for the Committee, but the tasks of the Swedish Committee were much wider than those of the Panel – the Committee covered any question of interest on the stock market. Another body of private law of importance for market behaviour was – and still is – the Swedish Securities Committee (the *Aktiemarknadsnämnden, AMN*), which was formed in the 1980s. We will come back to these committees in paragraph 135 *infra*.

129. Important legislative acts concerning the securities market are the Financial Instruments Trading Act from 1991 and the Securities Market Act from 2007. The former Act has been dealt with above in connection with public issue requirements (see paragraphs 56 et seq. *supra*). The latter Act is the result of the Markets in Financial Instruments Directive (MiFID). This Act is divided into five parts. After a part with introductory rules, the second part contains rules on the securities business, the third rules on the stock exchange and the fourth rules on clearing activities. The fifth and last part contains rules that are of common importance for the whole securities market. The intention behind this legislation is to harmonize the rules according to what follows from the MiFID. Thus, the Securities Market Act of

2007 gives the necessary basic rules for and on control of enterprises in the securities market, whether they are Swedish or from other countries. Where the abovementioned directive opens an area up for national regulation – that is, on questions concerning documentation, transaction reporting, and postponement of certain publications – it is usually the Financial Supervisory Authority that is responsible for the Swedish regulation.

130. In addition, the 2005 Act on Market Misuse establishes penalties for insider trading and market value manipulation. Any person who has obtained insider information and who, either by him/herself or by provoking someone else, uses this information while doing business on the securities market shall be punished (section 2). Undue influence on the market is also punishable according to section 8.

131. Of interest in this connection is the 2000 Notification Obligation Act on holdings of financial instruments. Persons with insight positions must notify the Financial Supervisory Authority of their holdings of shares in stock market companies. Insight positions are held by, *inter alia*, persons in leading and auditing positions in the company and its parent company and sometimes also in its subsidiary, as well as by other persons in higher positions or with other qualified tasks if they are in a position where they might receive information that could influence the value of the shares of the company. Also, shareholders who alone or together with certain other natural or artificial persons hold at least 10% of either the equity or the votes in the company are seen as persons with insight positions. To the shares owned by such persons are to be added shares owned by such persons' close relatives and artificial persons over which they have influence. All persons with insight positions must in principle see to it that their holdings are reported to the Swedish Financial Supervisory Authority, which is required to maintain an insight register, based on reports made in accordance with the Notification Obligation Act. This register, which is computerized, is public.

The companies themselves are also obliged to maintain registers concerning persons in higher positions or with other qualified tasks who are in a position where they might receive information that could influence the value of the shares of the company.

132. See paragraph 58 *supra* regarding the obligation for shareholders to disclose acquisitions of shares or votes when certain threshold values are passed.

133. Consumer protection is the aim of the Act of 2003 on Financial Advices for Consumers.

134. Also of some interest in this connection is the 2009 Act on measures against money laundering and financing of terrorism.

135. The Companies Act does not contain any rules on takeovers. Questions related to takeovers have instead for several decades been a task for the Swedish Industry and Commerce Stock Exchange Committee (the *Näringslivets börskommitté, NBK*) together with the Swedish Securities Committee (the *Aktiemarknadsnämnden, AMN*), which are both bodies of private law. The NBK issued a recommendation concerning public takeovers in 1971 that was later revised a number of times. The AMN, on the other hand, has made *in casu* announcements on how NBK recommendations should be understood when asked to state its opinion in connection with different buyouts. The NBK rules were made binding by means of different contractual devices. However, through the 2006 Act on Public Takeover Bids on the Stock Market (*lag* 2006:451 *om offentliga uppköpserbjudanden på aktiemarknaden*), Sweden has now implemented Directive 2004/25/EC of the European Parliament and the European Council of 21 April 2004 on takeover bids. This Act combines legislation and self-regulation. It states that all Swedish stock exchanges have to develop rules on public takeover bids that are in accord with the demands of Directive 2004/25/EC and that are also suitable. Exceptions to the rules may be allowed *in casu*. Public takeover bids involving shares in Swedish companies (and non-Swedish companies that are covered by the Act) may be made only by someone who has made a commitment to follow the rules of the stock market and to accept the sanctions that the stock market may decide.

Public takeover bids are supervised by the Swedish Financial Supervisory Authority. The Authority shall see to it that what the Act contains on duties of the offeror, on the obligation to launch a bid, on information to the employees, on defence operations, and so on are followed. The Act contains sanctions that the Authority may use. Interpretation of the rules and exceptions to them can be decided not only by the Authority, but also by a body representing industry and commerce. This rule makes it possible to keep the proximity to the market and maintain the competence that the AMN has developed during the many years it has been active in this area (see paragraph 128 *supra*). This means, however, that the body referred to in the Act also has public law obligations, and the Act states in some detail to what degree this body has to follow norms of public law.

The bidder is obliged to inform the Financial Supervisory Authority of his/her offer and the commitments he/she has made towards the stock exchange. This has to have been done when the offer is launched, at the latest.

The bidder is also obliged to issue a – for the takeover specific – document. The minimum standard of this document follows the regulation in Chapter 2a of the Financial Instruments Trading Act. For instance, the documents shall contain all the information that is necessary to enable the holders of the offeree company's securities to reach a properly informed decision on the bid (Chapter 2a, section 2). In case the payment consists of securities in the biding company, the information must also include such information that must be given in a prospectus (Chapter 2a, section 3).

As soon as the Financial Supervisory Authority (or, when this is permitted, the appropriate authority of another country) has approved and registered the offer document, the document shall be made public by the bidder. If the bidder has his/her domicile in Sweden, he/she must also inform the employees of the offeree company (the Act on Public Takeover Bids on the Stock Market Act, Chapter 4, section 1).

But the Act on public takeover bids states also that a natural or legal person must, as a result of the acquisition of securities of a company with its shares on a regulated market, sometimes also make a bid on the remaining shares in the company. This obligation is normally arrived at when the holdings of the acquirer – including the holdings of closely related legal and/or natural persons – represent 30% of the total number of votes of the company. However, exemption may be granted for special reasons. (No obligation to make a bid exists when someone reaches the 30% level through a bid on all the shares of a company.)

The Act on public takeover bids on the stock market also covers rules on protection against takeover bids. The Act states that the board of directors is not allowed to take any protective action unless the general meeting of the attacked company has made such a decision. However, the board is nonetheless allowed to try to find alternative offers. And an exception may also be granted.

The rules on breakthrough in Directive 2004/25/EC (Article 11) have not been adopted by the Swedish legislature. If the owners of a Swedish company wish to adopt such rules for their own company, they are, however, free to do so on the condition that the decision is supported by all shareholders present at the general meeting and also that these shareholders together represent not less than nine-tenths of all shares of the company.

The Act on public takeovers does not contain any rules on the buyout of minority shareholders. The rules in Chapter 22 of the Companies Act (see paragraphs 255 et seq. *infra*) have been deemed to be sufficient.

XI. Warrants and Convertible Instruments

136. As noted earlier, the Companies Act contains rules on warrants and convertible instruments.

An issue of convertible instruments can be attractive to a company as an alternative to a new issue when it might be doubtful whether the market is willing to subscribe for new shares. Such instruments combine for the subscriber the advantages of lent capital with a right to both a fixed rate of interest, rather than a dividend dependent on a decision by the general meeting, and often repayment when the loan is due and with the possibility of sharing in the higher value of the company's shares if their value should increase. And for the issuing company, it has the advantage that the interest on the loan might be lower than would otherwise have been the case.

Also a warrant can – but must not – be combined with a company loan.

These two kinds of instruments were introduced in Sweden in 1973 to assist a very weak market.

137. The Financial Instruments (Accounts) Act provides that warrants and convertible instruments may be registered pursuant to that Act. See on this Act paragraphs 123 et seq. *supra*.

A. Warrants

138. An increase of the share capital through the device of warrants is done in two steps. First, a decision to issue warrants is made. This decision has no influence on the size of the share capital, but is the base for the second phase, when the holders of warrants can use their warrants to subscribe for shares.

139. The decision to issue warrants is normally made by the general meeting with absolute majority (Chapter 11, section 2). Data and documentation for the decision by the general meeting (including a proposal on the exact wording of the proposed decision) must be issued (Chapter 14, sections 4–9). Where the issue resolution requires alteration of the articles of association (e.g., concerning the size of the share capital), such fact should be mentioned. The decision must also state any rules on issues in kind or setoffs and other special conditions (Chapter 14, section 9). The decision to issue warrants is followed by subscription, allotment and registration.

140. The board can decide on an issue of warrants subject to the approval of the general meeting. And the general meeting can decide to authorize the board to issue warrants. Such an authorization can, as a maximum, be given for a period ending before the opening of the next annual general meeting. Such an authorization may include a right for the board to deviate from the preferential rights of earlier shareholders. In public companies, however, the board may never decide on such deviations in favour of the persons referred to in paragraph 47 *supra.*

141. With regard to the preferential rights to warrants of earlier shareholders, the rules are the same as those to new issues: The general clauses are applicable, and the preferential rights of earlier shareholders may not be set aside unless the warrants shall be paid for with non-cash consideration *or* the pre-emption right shall be governed in another manner as a consequence of (a) a provision in the articles of association such as that referred to in Chapter 4, section 3; (b) terms and conditions of an earlier issue of warrants or convertibles instruments; or (c) provisions of the issue resolution (Chapter 14, section 1). A decision to set aside the preferential right in the last case requires a majority of at least two-thirds both of the votes cast and of the shares represented at the meeting (Chapter 14, section 2). When the decision is made in a public company or a subsidiary to such a company and directs the issue to the categories mentioned in paragraph 47 *supra*, then the decision must be made at a general meeting and receive the support of nine-tenths both of the votes and of the shares represented at the meeting. See the Companies Act, Chapter 16.

142. The decision to issue warrants is followed by subscription, allotment and registration.

143. As to the second phase, the terms and conditions of the issue must state the amount by which the share capital might be increased, the amount to be paid for each new share, when the warrant may be used and the time when dividends on the new shares shall be declared (Companies Act, Chapter 14, section 6).

If the holder of a warrant decides to subscribe for shares according to his/her warrant, this is usually made on a subscription list; in a CDS company, subscription might be made through payment. The decision data and information that the subscriber must be given are stated in detail in Chapter 14, section 32.

144. If the subscription is valid, the holder of the warrant has an absolute right to get the number of shares that he/she is entitled to according to his/her warrant. The shares shall immediately be registered in the share register and also be paid. The payment must not be below the quotient value of the earlier shares; capital contributed in kind and setoff are not permitted at this stage (with a certain exception concerning setoff in public companies). See the Companies Act, Chapter 14, sections 37 et seq. and sections 46 et seq.

145. The board of directors has to report for registration the number of shares issued as the result of the subscription and paid for in full (Chapter 14, section 43). This must be done not later than three months after the end of the period for subscription for new shares. However, where the subscription period lasts more than one year, the report has to be submitted not later than three months after the end of each financial year during which subscription has taken place.

Registration is barred unless the shares have been paid for in full. Upon registration, the share capital is increased by the total amount of the reported shares.

B. Convertible Instruments

146. A convertible instrument contains a promise by the company to the creditor that he/she is entitled to convert the whole or part of his/her claim into shares in the company. Sometimes, however, the creditor has not only a right, but also an obligation to convert his/her claim into shares.

147. The terms of conversion for new shares are to be so determined that conversion can be effected without an amendment of the articles of association. That means *en clair* that when a decision is made to issue convertible instruments, there must be enough room left in the maximum share capital according to the articles of association (see paragraph 26 *supra*) for shares that might be issued for converted debt. If necessary, the articles of association must therefore first be amended. The conversion price must not be lower than such an amount that the company, following conversion, has received a consideration, which, with respect to each share provided in exchange, corresponds to not less than the quotient value of earlier shares unless the difference is covered by cash upon conversion.

148. The decision to issue convertible instruments is normally made by the general meeting with absolute majority (Chapter 11, section 2). Data and documentation for the decision by the general meeting (including a proposal on the exact wording of the proposed decision) must be issued (Chapter 15, sections 4–8).

The decision must also state any rules on issues in kind or setoffs and other special conditions (Chapter 15, section 9).

149. The board can decide on an issue of convertible instruments subject to the approval of the general meeting. And the general meeting may decide to authorize the board to issue such instruments. Such an authorization can, as a maximum, be given for a period ending prior to the next annual general meeting. Such an authorization may include a right for the board to deviate from the preferential right of old shareholders. In public companies, however, the board may never decide on such deviations in favour of the persons referred to in paragraph 47 *supra*.

150. With regard to the preferential rights to convertible instruments of earlier shareholders, the rules are the same as those to new issues. The general clauses are applicable, and the preferential rights of earlier shareholders may not be set aside unless the convertible instruments shall be paid for with non-cash consideration *or* the pre-emption right shall be governed in another manner as a consequence of (a) a provision in the articles of association such as that referred to in Chapter 4, section 3; (b) terms and conditions of an earlier issue of warrants or convertible instruments; or (c) provisions of the issue resolution (Chapter 14, section 1). A decision to set aside the preferential right in the last case requires a majority of at least two-thirds both of the votes cast and of the shares represented at the meeting (Chapter 14, section 2). When the decision is made in a public company or a subsidiary to such a company and directs the issue to the categories mentioned in paragraph 47 *supra*, then the decision must be made at a general meeting and receive the support of nine-tenths both of the votes and of the shares represented at the meeting. See the Companies Act, Chapter 16.

Convertible instruments that are subscribed for shall be paid for in cash or with non-cash consideration, provided the issue contains a provision thereon. A debt due to subscription for a convertible instrument may be set off against a claim in a private company only where the issue contains a provision thereon. In a public company, the right to pay by way of setoff is less restricted.

If later the convertible instrument is converted into shares, the instrument should be provided with a notation stating that conversion has taken place. The new shares are registered in the share register.

151. The board of directors has to report for registration the number of shares that have been converted. This must be done not later than three months after the end of the conversion period. However, where the conversion period lasts more than one year, the report has to be submitted to the registration authority not later than three months after the end of each financial year during which conversions have taken place.

Registration is barred unless the shares have been paid for at the quotient value of the earlier shares. Upon registration, the share capital is increased by the total quotient value of the reported shares.

§3. SHAREHOLDERS, MANAGEMENT AND CONTROL

I. Introduction

152. There must be at least three and sometimes even four bodies (*organ* in Swedish terminology) in a company limited by shares: (1) a general meeting, traditionally seen as the highest internal body of the company; (2) a board of directors with responsibility for the organization of the company and the management of its activities; (3) a managing director – who is mandatory only in public companies, but who can also be appointed in other companies – with responsibility for the day-to-day management of the company; and (4) one or more auditors.

II. Shareholders' Meetings

A. *Starting Points*

153. As already noted, the Swedish Companies Act does not allow shares carrying no right to vote. But it is possible to issue different classes of shares with differing voting rights (with the ratio of 1:10 as a maximum; see paragraph 99 *supra*).

154. The shareholders' right to participate in company decision making is exercised at general meetings of shareholders (Chapter 7, section 1). If nothing else is stated, each shareholder who is registered in the share register is empowered to attend such meetings, to take part in the discussions there and to vote. See paragraphs 114 *supra* and 163 *infra*.

B. *Different Kinds of General Meeting*

155. Two forms of general meeting are provided for in the Companies Act: annual general meetings and extraordinary general meetings. An annual general meeting has to be held within six months of the end of each financial year, and, under Chapter 7, section 11, resolutions must be passed at that meeting with respect to (1) adoption of the income statement and the balance sheet, as well as, in some parents of a groups of enterprises, the consolidated income statement and the consolidated balance sheet; (2) approval of the company's profit or loss according to the adopted balance sheet; and (3) discharge (or non-discharge) from liability of the members of the board and the managing director. In a company whose shares are bought and sold on a regulated market in Sweden, the annual general meeting shall also adopt resolutions regarding guidelines for compensation to senior management (Chapter 7, section 61). Other matters to be dealt with at the annual general meeting follow from the articles of association – such as the election of directors and auditors. Additional matters may be put before the meeting by the board, the auditors or the shareholders.

As for the annual report of the company and profits and dividends, see paragraphs 61 et seq. *supra*.

It may be added that the articles of association may include provisions for more than one general meeting each year.

156. An extraordinary general meeting is to be held whenever the board of directors considers it appropriate. But such a meeting must also be held whenever it is requested for a specified purpose by an auditor or by the owners of one-tenth of all shares (Chapter 7, section 13).

C. Convening the Meeting

157. The convening of a general meeting is the responsibility of the board. Where a general meeting that is to be held pursuant to the Companies Act, the articles of association or a resolution adopted at a general meeting is not properly convened, the Companies Registration Office must, upon application by a director, the managing director, an auditor or a shareholder, immediately convene the meeting (Chapter 7, section 17).

158. As to notices of a general meeting, the rules are the following (Chapter 7, sections 18–20).

The starting point is that a notice shall be issued not earlier than six and not later than four weeks before the meeting. This is the case with both ordinary and extraordinary meetings when the issue is alteration of the articles of association. For other extraordinary general meetings, the maximum time is six weeks, and the minimum time is two weeks. As for private companies, the Companies Act accepts however that the articles of association state that notice shall be issued not less than two weeks before the meeting. But if there are no rules on this in the articles of association, the general rule applies. These rules are deemed to give the shareholders a fair chance to attend. But they – like other rules for the protection of minorities – can be ignored in one-man companies (and in companies where all the shareholders agree to ignore them).

Section 14 includes rules on continued general meetings, and section 22 covers notices when, according to the articles of association, a resolution must be adopted at two general meetings to be valid.

159. A general meeting must, according to Chapter 7, section 23, be convened pursuant to the articles of association. Written notice to each shareholder whose mailing address is known to the company is necessary, however, if an annual general meeting is to be held at a different time than that prescribed in the articles of association *or* if the general meeting is to consider matters concerning (1) an amendment of the articles of association that requires an extra qualified majority (see paragraph 170 *infra*); (2) the winding-up of the company; (3) a review of the liquidator's final report; or (4) whether the liquidation of the company shall cease.

In public companies, a notice to attend a general meeting must – in addition to what is stated in the previous paragraph – always be published in both the Official Gazette and not less than one daily newspaper stated in the articles of association.

159.1. In public companies with their shares listed on a regulated market or an equivalent market outside the EEA, the following should be added to the text in the two preceding paragraphs: The minimum time for the convening of the general meeting is three weeks and the convening must be published both in the *Official Gazette* and at the website of the company. Information must also be sent to the shareholders according to what is stated in the Act, and a notice must also be published in a daily newspaper stated in the articles of association. The information must include all relevant information concerning the meeting to be held. See Chapter 7, section 56 a.

159.2. Electronic devices may be used in some public companies in order to inform the shareholders of meetings (Chapter 7, sections 64 et seq.).

160. With regard to public companies with their shares listed on a regulated market or on an equivalent market outside the EEA, the notice shall also include information on the total number of shares and votes in the company and, where relevant, how many of these shares that are owned by the company itself (Chapter 7, section 63). The notice shall also contain information concerning the website where information can be found concerning proxies, voting by mail, documents submitted to the meeting and the right of the shareholders to request information at the meeting (same section).

161. The notice to attend shall contain a proposed agenda for the general meeting. In the proposed agenda, the board of directors shall clearly state the matters to be addressed at the general meeting. The matters must be numbered. Where the meeting is to deal with an amendment of the articles of association, the notice must describe the essential contents of the proposed amendment.

162. General meetings must be held in the municipality where the registered office of the board of directors is located unless the articles of association provide that the meeting shall or may be held at another specifically mentioned place in Sweden (Chapter 7, section 15). Only where extraordinary circumstances – such as a war – make it necessary may the general meeting be held elsewhere.

163. To facilitate preparation of the voting list and other formalities connected with the holding of the general meeting, the articles of association may provide that a shareholder must give the company notice of his/her intention to attend the general meeting not later than the day stated in the notice convening the meeting. This day must not be more than five days before the meeting. See the Companies Act, Chapter 7, section 2.

A problem of a similar but nevertheless another kind is the impossibility of providing a share register for a CSD company (paragraph 122 *supra*) as of the date of the general meeting. Complications connected with this have led to the rule (Chapter 7, section 2) that in such companies any person entitled to attend a general meeting as a shareholder must be listed as such in a transcript of the share register five days before the shareholders' general meeting. This means that a person who has become a shareholder during the last few days before the meeting cannot attend.

(A person who is recorded on the list, but who has sold his/her shares during the days preceding the general meeting, is supposed to have lost the right to attend, since he/she is not then a shareholder.)

163.1. The articles of association can allow the shareholders to send their votes in advance by mail (Chapter 7, section 4 a).

164. A shareholder may exercise his/her rights at a general meeting not only personally, but also through a representative, who must be in possession of a written and dated proxy. The proxy remains valid for no more than one year from its date of issue (Chapter 7, section 3).

In CSD companies the shareholders have however the right to use not only one but two representatives. In such companies, the proxies may remain valid for up to five years (same section).

Another kind of proxy is a proxy form that the company's board of directors may provide the shareholders (with yes and no alternatives to the issues stated) (Chapter 7, section 4). Such proxy forms must be sent to the shareholders in all public companies with their shares on a regulated market or an equivalent market outside the EEA (Chapter 7, section 54a).

D. The Agenda

165. The general meeting has certain exclusive powers, such as the three (in some companies, four) above-mentioned resolutions that have to be passed at the annual general meeting (paragraph 155 *supra*), resolutions to increase the share capital through bonus issues and to decrease the capital (unless perhaps the articles provide that the share capital may be reduced by a redemption of shares) and resolutions to wind up the company or to wind it up in combination with a merger or de-merger. Normally, directors are also elected at general meetings, and at least one of the auditors has to be elected in the same way.

166. To increase the power of the board of directors at the expense of the general meeting, the Companies Act states that the general meeting may not normally declare a dividend higher than the dividend proposed or approved by the board (Chapter 18, section 1), nor can it decide on a reduction of the share capital involving a repayment to the shareholders unless the board has given a statement in writing as to whether the proposed repayment is justifiable in light of the prudence rule (Chapter 20, section 8).

As stated above, new issues of shares and issues of warrants and convertible instruments are basically within the power of the general meeting, but the meeting may authorize the board to make such decisions. As for restrictions on this possibility in public companies, see paragraphs 47, 140 and 149 *supra*.

167. Apart from what follows from the Companies Act as such, the articles of association may extend the power of the general meeting, as can resolutions adopted by the general meeting itself.

A more difficult question to answer is to what degree matters of particularly great importance to the company must be decided by the general meeting. One – insufficient – answer to this is that if there is no reason to believe that the general meeting would object to the way a matter is decided by the board, it should not be necessary for the board to consult the general meeting.

Finally, it should be added that the general meeting may not exert an influence over the board that makes it impossible for the board to act as a body with responsibility for the organization of the company and the management of its activities.

E. Rules on General Meetings

168. As for the holding of the general meeting as such, the Companies Act sets out certain basic rules – concerning the chairman of the meeting, the voting list, the minutes and how they are to be preserved for the future, and so on. For the rest, normal meeting formalities and procedures should be followed.

168.1. In public companies with their shares listed on a regulated market or an equivalent market outside the EEA, any shareholder has the right to demand that the protocol from the meeting shall contain specific information concerning the result of the voting. The protocol must also be published at the website of the company (Chapter 7, section 68.).

169. According to the Companies Act, Chapter 7, section 40, a resolution of the general meeting of shareholders is normally passed by a simple (absolute) majority vote and, in the event of a tie, by the casting vote of the chairman of the meeting. In an election, however, the candidate receiving the largest number of votes – which is not necessarily an overall majority – is to be considered elected (Chapter 7, section 41). In the event of a tie, the election is to be decided by drawing lots unless the general meeting decides prior to the election that a new vote shall be held in the event of a tied vote. (This shall not apply where otherwise prescribed in the articles of association, which may not, however, prescribe that a valid election requires more votes than stated in Chapter 7, section 41.)

170. There are, however, certain decisions where the majority needed is higher than stated in paragraph 169. This is, for example, the case for amendments of the articles of association. Normally, such amendments are valid if the shareholders in favour of the amendment represent two-thirds both of the votes cast and of the shares represented at the meeting (Chapter 7, section 42). As for amendments to the articles of association that, with regard to shares already issued, reduce the shareholders' rights to the company's profits or other assets, restrict the right to acquire shares in the company and/or alter the legal relationship between the shares, a larger qualified majority is required: Attending shareholders representing nine-tenths of all shares must vote in favour of the resolution.

As for amendments that limit the number of votes that a shareholder may cast at a general meeting require that a larger amount of the net profit for the financial year be kept in the company or regulate distribution of the profits or remaining assets in connection with the winding-up of the company in a particular way, the majority required is two-thirds of the votes cast and nine-tenths of the shares represented at the meeting. When a curtailment of shareholders' rights concerns only certain shares or a particular class of shares, a larger qualified majority is required only with reference to the shares concerned (Chapter 7, sections 43–45).

171. Amendments to the articles of association are not the only decisions that require a qualified majority, however. There are also other situations in which the Companies Act states that a decision is to be made by more than simple majority. The Act lists these cases in Chapter 7, section 40.

172. It should finally be mentioned that the articles of association may prescribe that the permission of the government is necessary for an amendment to be made (Chapter 3, section 6).

F. Minority Protection

173. The rules discussed above, which offer quite good protection for the majority, should be seen in the light of the following rules, which are intended to protect individual shareholders and the minority.

174. A shareholder (or a person representing the shareholder by proxy) attending the general meeting has a mandatory right to be accompanied by two advisers, for example, an accountant and an attorney (Chapter 7, section 5).

175. A shareholder may vote for all the shares owned or represented by him/her unless otherwise prescribed in the articles of association (Chapter 7, section 8).

176. As for bias, the Companies Act, Chapter 7, section 46, provides that no shareholder may vote personally or by proxy with respect to (1) any legal action against himself/herself, (2) his/her discharge from liability for damages or other obligations towards the company, or (3) any legal action or discharge from liability as referred to under (1) and (2) concerning someone else if the shareholder has a material interest in the matter contrary to that of the company. This also applies to shareholders' representatives.

177. Any shareholder is entitled to have a matter dealt with at a general meeting, provided that the board of directors has received his/her request in time to have the matter included in the notice convening the meeting (Chapter 7, section 16).

178. Where provisions of the Companies Act or the articles of association regarding notice of a general meeting or the furnishing of documents at such a meeting have been disregarded concerning a particular matter, the meeting may not pass a resolution on that matter without the consent of the shareholders affected by the error unless the matter has to be dealt with at the meeting pursuant to law or the articles of association or is directly connected with another matter on which a resolution is to be passed. The general meeting may also resolve that an extraordinary general meeting shall be convened to address the matter (Chapter 7, section 26).

179. The shareholders also have a right under the Companies Act, Chapter 7, sections 32–36, to demand information at the general meeting concerning any circumstance that may affect the assessment of a matter on the agenda and any circumstance that may affect the assessment of the company's financial position (the latter right, however, arises in public companies only at general meetings where the annual report is to be discussed; Chapter 7, section 57). If the company is part of a group, the duty to provide information also extends to the company's relations with other group companies and, if the company is the parent in the group, the group's accounts, as well as information with a bearing on the examination of the different subsidiaries' financial positions to the extent that these concern the parent's position.

But – and this is an important point – if the board is of the opinion that the information thus requested cannot be given to the shareholders without material prejudice to the company, the information shall, if the shareholder so demands, instead be given to the auditor of the company, who in turn has to make a written statement to the board as to whether the information would have given rise to an amendment of the audit report or whether in other respects it occasions critical comment. This statement must be sent by the board to the shareholder who requested the information and be kept available by the board for other shareholders.

In small companies – that is, companies with ten or fewer shareholders – the shareholders have a greater right to information. Here every shareholder, as well any shareholder's representative or adviser, has a right to acquaint himself/herself with the books, accounts and other documents concerning the activities of the company to the extent that this is required to form an opinion on the state and results of the company or on a certain item of business to be transacted at a general meeting of shareholders. At the request of the shareholder, the board of directors and the managing director must also provide him/her with such detailed statements and copies of documents as are required for the said purposes, provided that this can be done without unreasonable cost or inconvenience. These requirements do not apply, however, if giving information to the shareholder on the activities of the company would involve an obvious risk of serious harm to the company.

180. As a last means of protection for individual shareholders and the minority, Chapter 7, section 47, of the Companies Act contains a general clause that states that a general meeting may not pass any resolution that is likely to give undue advantage to a shareholder or another person to the detriment of the company or other shareholders.

181. To this it should be added, however, that the general meeting has to adhere to the articles of association and their provisions regarding the kind of business activities that the company may engage in. If the articles do not state otherwise, the general meeting should, furthermore, adhere to activities that are in line with the company's purpose of making profits for its shareholders.

182. If a resolution by a general meeting has not been properly passed or if a resolution is otherwise contrary to the Companies Act, the Annual Reports Act or the articles of association, a shareholder, the board of directors, a director or the managing director may take legal action against the company for the annulment or amendment of the resolution (Chapter 7, section 50). Such action may also be brought by a person whom the board has improperly refused to enter as a shareholder in the share register.

Such action shall be instituted within three months of the date of the resolution. Otherwise, the right to bring an action is usually lost unless, for example, the resolution passed was contrary to Companies Act rules for the protection of creditors and other third parties. If this is the case, the decision is in principle a nullity. 'In principle' is used here because a merger plan or a de-merger plan becomes definitely binding six months after its adoption (Chapter 7, section 51; Chapter 23, section 52; Chapter 24, section 30).

III. Management of a Company

183. The Swedish Companies Act contains rules on two management 'bodies': the board of directors, which is a mandatory body in all companies, and the managing director, a position that is mandatory only in public companies, but that can also exist in other companies.

A. *Board of Directors*

184. Every company limited by shares has to have a board of directors (Chapter 8, section 1). In private companies, this board may consist of only one member, provided that there is at least one deputy director elected. There is nothing, however, to prevent such companies from having boards consisting of more directors. In public companies, the board must consist of at least three members (without any requirement that there be deputy directors).

1. Appointment

185. The board is elected by the general meeting unless the articles of association provide that directors are to be appointed by other means. It is possible in a private company to have all directors appointed outside the general meeting, but in public companies, at least more than half of the members of the board of directors shall be appointed by the general meeting (Chapter 8, sections 8 and 47). Employee representatives are appointed in addition to the number thus elected or appointed. See concerning these representatives paragraph 227 *infra*.

186. The term of office of directors other than those representing the employees is one year, but may be specified for a longer period in the articles of association;

however, it may not exceed four years. There is nothing to prevent a director from being re-elected (Chapter 8, section 13).

187. A legal person may not be a member of the board of directors (Chapter 8, section 10).

188. At least half the directors must be residents of the EEA unless special permission is obtained from the Companies Registration Office (Chapter 8, section 9). A person under age, in bankruptcy or with a custodian pursuant to the Parental Code may not be a director. The same applies to a person who has been declared subject to an incapacity to engage in trade (Chapter 8, section 11).

189. The term of office of a director can expire prematurely at the request of the director concerned or of the body that has appointed him/her (Chapter 8, section 14).

190. The remuneration payable to the directors must be decided by the general meeting (Chapter 8, section 23a).

In a company whose shares are bought and sold on a regulated market in Sweden, the board shall annually propose guidelines for decisions regarding salary and other compensation for the managing director and other persons in the company's management. Transfers of securities and options to acquire securities from the company in the future shall be equated with compensation. See Chapter 8, sections 51–54; see also paragraph 155 *supra.*

2. Formalities

191. As for formalities, the Companies Act, in Chapter 8, sections 46a and 46b, lays down certain basic rules for the board of a public company. The board must – except in companies with only one director – each year issue a formal work plan for its work, and it must further issue instructions regarding allocation of work between the different company organs. The intent of these rules is to make it clear *both* which board member is responsible for what within the board *and* also which organ and/or body inside the greater structure – with board, managing director, divisions and other persons – is responsible for what. The goal of these rules is to make it easier to hold someone responsible when questions of responsibility and liability arise.

192. The Companies Act lays also down certain basic rules on the chairman of the board (Chapter 8, section 17), on how he/she is chosen and on his/her obligation to ensure that the board performs the duties mentioned in paragraph 191 and also that board meetings are held. The board must under all circumstances be convened by the chairman at the request of a director or the managing director. The Act states further that minutes must be taken and preserved in a secure manner.

The Companies Act states that a quorum exists when more than half of the directors – or such higher number as is prescribed in the articles of association – are present (Chapter 8, section 21). However, no matter may be decided unless, as far as possible, all directors have had the opportunity to participate in its consideration and have also received sufficient material on which to base a decision. Where a director is unable to attend and a deputy director is available as a substitute, the deputy shall be given the opportunity to attend.

As for what majority is needed for different decisions made by the board, a simple (absolute) majority is the normal rule. The chairman has the deciding vote in case of a tie. If not all the directors are present, those voting in favour must nevertheless be more than one-third of all directors unless otherwise provided in the articles of association (Chapter 8, section 22).

3. Duties

193. The board of directors is responsible for the organization of the company and the management of its affairs (Chapter 8, section 4). If no managing director has been appointed, this responsibility has no limitations. It is particularly mentioned in the Act that the board has to see to it that the organization of accounting and the management of assets includes a satisfactory element of control. This would have been the law anyway, but the statement was included in the Act to prevent any board from believing that these were the responsibilities of the auditor(s) of the company.

193.1. In public companies with their shares on a regulated market, the board must nominate an auditing committee unless the board can itself monitor the duties that such a committee has to carry out. These duties include the control the financial reports of the company and its internal control. The members of the committee must continuously keep in touch with the auditor of the company and discuss relevant questions with him/her. The committee must in particular see to the impartiality and independence of the auditor (Chapter 8, section 49 a.).

194. The board of directors represents the company and signs for it (Chapter 8, section 35).

195. However, according to the Companies Act, Chapter 8, section 27, the board may also authorize a director, a managing director or someone else to represent the company and sign for it with the same authority as the board itself unless such delegation of authority is prohibited by the articles of association. The board may stipulate that the right to represent the company and sign for it must be exercised by two or more persons jointly. Such persons authorized to sign for the company (*firmatecknare*) are very common in Swedish companies. They are registered as such at the Companies Registration Office.

4. Limits on Competence

196. The board of directors is bound by the Companies Act, the Annual Reports Act, the articles of association and directives from the general meeting, although the last are binding only on the condition that they are not invalid because they are contrary to the Companies Act, the Annual Reports Act, the articles of association (Companies Act, Chapter 8, section 42) or criminal law.

197. It follows from the Companies Act, Chapter 8, section 41, that the board of directors may not enter into legal transactions or undertake other measures that are likely to give undue advantage to a shareholder or a third party to the detriment of the company or other shareholders. This 'general clause' is similar to the general clause on decisions by the general meeting (paragraph 180 *supra*).

198. To this, it should be added that the board of directors has to adhere to the articles of association and their provisions regarding the kind of business activities that the company is to engage in. If the articles do not state otherwise, the board of directors should, moreover, do business with the intention of making profits for the shareholders.

199. The Companies Act, in Chapter 8, section 23, deals with bias. It states that a director may not deal with matters relating to agreements between himself/herself and the company. But a director is also prohibited from dealing with matters relating to agreements between the company and a third party if the director has a material interest in the matter that is contrary to that of the company. A director is further prohibited from participating in any agreement between the company and a legal person that the board member is entitled to represent, whether alone or together with another person. This last part of the section can make it impossible for persons to be members of several boards if the different companies they represent enter into agreements with each other.

However, it is only when the director is personally affected that he/she is disqualified from dealing with a matter on the grounds of possible bias. For that reason, the bias stated for persons representing legal persons does not apply where the board member owns all of the shares in the company, whether directly or indirectly through a legal person, *or* where the party contracting with the company is an undertaking in the same group or in a group of undertakings of a corresponding nature.

It should finally be added that court actions and other legal actions rank alongside agreements with regard to bias.

200. If a company has only one shareholder, any contract between him/her and the company that does not concern day-to-day transactions on normal conditions shall be either stated in or attached to the minutes of the board.

201. What, then, if the board has acted contrary to the rules of the Companies Act, the articles of association or the directives of the general meeting?

If the board has acted contrary to the powers that it can hold according to the Companies Act, the company will not be bound. The board cannot, for example, make decisions that are the preserve of the general meeting. If, on the other hand, the board has acted contrary to minority protection rules in the Companies Act – such as the rule against bias or the general clause (see paragraph 197 *supra*) – then the company is bound unless it shows that the other party to the transaction realized or should have realized that the board was exceeding its authority. Finally, acts infringing rules in the articles of association – for example, on the activities of the company – or contravening directives from the general meeting cannot be invalidated according to the Companies Act. They bind the company (Chapter 8, section 42).

202. This raises the question of what protection the shareholders are given by all the rules described above. The answer is that their protection is weak for several reasons. First, it is most unlikely that the shareholders will receive any information about acts that the board of directors has undertaken contrary to the rules it is supposed to follow. But if the shareholders do receive such information, what can they do? The answer is that they can, if they are in the majority, dismiss any director or at least refrain from re-electing him/her. And they might (possibly even if they are in the minority) institute an action for damages under the rules of the Companies Act (Chapter 29, sections 1 and 7) against the directors, should the company or they themselves have incurred loss because of the acts of the board of directors. The cost associated with an action for damages – which will be borne by the shareholder(s) if the action is unsuccessful – will in fact prevent most such litigation.

203. It should be added that what has been said in paragraphs 196–201 *supra* also applies to the *firmatecknare*, see paragraph 195 *supra*, with the possible exception that acts contrary to a rule in the articles of association or to directives of the general meeting or the board of directors might not be invalidated if the company shows that the other party to the transaction realized or should have realized that the *firmatecknare* was exceeding his/her authority. It should also be added that the Companies Act does not contain any rules concerning damages payable either to the company or to individual shareholders in the case of harm caused by a *firmatecknare.*

B. Managing Director

204. Let us now turn to the managing director (*den verkställande direktören*).

1. Appointment

205. Every public company must have a managing director. In other companies, a managing director may be appointed. This director is appointed by the board of directors, which is consequently above him/her in the internal hierarchy of the company.

206. The managing director must be a resident of the EEA unless a special exemption is granted. A person who is under age, is in bankruptcy or has a custodian pursuant to the Parental Code may not be the managing director. Nor may a person who has been declared subject to an incapacity to engage in trade become the managing director (Chapter 8, sections 30 and 31).

207. The managing director is to some degree regarded as an employee of the company, and his/her relationship with the company is also regulated by labour law.

The Security of Employment Act, however, does not normally apply to managing directors – the board can get rid of a managing director without following the strict rules of that Act. On the other hand, such a dismissal may prove expensive for the company if it is without cause.

2. Duties

208. Under the Companies Act, Chapter 8, section 29, the managing director is in charge of the day-to-day management of the company, in accordance with guidelines and instructions laid down by the board. The line between questions that have to be decided by the board and those within the sphere of the managing director is not always very easy to draw, but it has not been the legislature's intention to transfer to the managing director matters that are of great importance with regard to the scope of the company's activities or that are unusual with regard to the nature of the company's activities – looked upon in the light of the activities mentioned in the articles of association. But such matters, too, may be decided by the managing director when waiting for a resolution of the board would result in considerable inconvenience to the company. The managing director is responsible in particular for ensuring that accounting records are kept in accordance with the law and that assets are managed in a secure manner.

209. The managing director is always authorized to represent the company and sign for it with regard to measures that are his/her responsibility under section 29 (see Chapter 8, section 36).

3. Limits on Competence

210. A managing director must follow not only the directives issued by the general meeting, but also those issued by the board of directors, provided that they are not contrary to the Companies Act, the Annual Reports Act, the articles of association or criminal law (the Companies Act, Chapter 8, section 41, paragraph 2).

211. The general clause prohibiting legal transactions or other measures likely to give undue advantage to a shareholder or a third party to the detriment of the company or other shareholders is as relevant to a managing director as it is to directors. And so are the nature of the company's activities and its purpose, as well as situations where a managing director could be biased. See paragraphs 197–199 *supra*.

212. When a managing director has acted contrary to such directives as mentioned above, the third party is in the same position as if he/she had acted contrary to the rules (see paragraph 201 *supra*). A special subsection, however, covers the situation where the managing director goes beyond the day-to-day activities of the company. If the managing director has exceeded his/her authority according to that section of the Companies Act, the company is not bound if it is able to show that the other party realized or should have realized that the managing director was exceeding his/ her authority. Otherwise, the company is bound (see Chapter 8, section 42).

213. As for the position of the shareholders when a managing director has exceeded his/her authority, their main alternatives are to exert pressure on the board to get rid of the managing director and to have him/her pay damages either to the company or to themselves. Neither alternative is normally very effective.

4. Special Agents for Service of Process

214. It should finally be added that the chapter of the Companies Act dealing with the management of a company prescribes (in Chapter 8, section 40) that in case the company has no authorized representative who is a resident in Sweden, the board of directors shall authorize a person who is resident in Sweden to act as agent for service of process on behalf of the company. Such a person is called special agent for service of process (*särskild delgivningsmottagare*).

IV. Auditors

215. The last regular 'body' of a Swedish company is the auditor or auditors.

215.1. The Companies Act was, as of 1 November 2010, amended in order to allow small-sized private companies to refrain from being audited. The amendment was made with the purpose to reduce the administrative and economic burdens of small enterprises. Such a decision must be taken by the general meeting and takes effect through an amendment of the articles of association.

The text that now follows on auditors and auditing is based on the assumption that that there are auditors in a company.

A. Appointment Etc.

216. An auditor is traditionally seen as a means of protecting the owners of an organization whose management the owners are not allowed to monitor themselves.

There are two main reasons why the owners are not allowed to perform such monitoring: (1) They might in reality be competitors of the company, and (2) their supervisory activities could cause too much interference with the internal organization of the company (see, however, paragraph 179 *supra in fine*). Instead, they have the right to elect one or more auditors whose task is to perform the necessary monitoring on their behalf. As a consequence, the Companies Act states, in Chapter 9, section 8, that at least one auditor must be elected by the general meeting. If several auditors are to be appointed in the same company, the articles of association may provide that one or more of them are to be appointed in some other manner. As time has passed, the auditor has also come to be entrusted with seeing to the interests of parties dependent on the company: individual shareholders, creditors, employees, state and local government, and so on. The legislative history of the Companies Act, together with various sections of the Act itself, shows that it was the intention of the legislature that auditors should be under an obligation to see to the interests of these other parties as well.

B. Qualifications and Independence

217. To ensure sound auditing, it is necessary to have competent auditors. The basic requirement for anyone who was to act as an auditor of a Swedish company is that he/she has the requisite knowledge of and experience in accounting and financial matters to perform the task, considering the nature and extent of the operations of the company (Companies Act, Chapter 9, section 11). However, this requirement proved to be too vague, and following a reform in the early 1980s, every Swedish company had to have at least one auditor appointed by the general meeting who was either an authorized public accountant (*auktoriserad revisor*) or an approved public accountant (*godkänd revisor*). But nowadays only an authorized public accountant or an approved public accountant is allowed to act as auditor in a company – public or private (Companies Act, Chapter 9, section 12). Sometimes, however, an approved public accountant is not enough – in that case, at least one of the auditors appointed by the general meeting shall be an authorized public accountant. This is the case where (1) the company satisfies more than one of the following conditions: (a) the median number of employees of the company during each of the two most recent financial years has exceeded fifty, (b) the company's reported balance sheet total for each of the two most recent financial years has exceeded SEK 40 million, and (c) the company's reported net turnover for each of the two most recent years has exceeded SEK 80 million; *or* (2) the company's shares, warrants or debentures are bought and sold on a regulated market or an equivalent market outside the EEA (Chapter 9, section 13). The same applies to the parent of a group of companies where the group satisfies more than one of the above-mentioned three conditions in item (1) (Chapter 9, section 14). (In some situations, with special permission, an approved public accountant may replace an authorized public accountant, Chapter 9, section 15.)

A person under age, in bankruptcy or with a custodian pursuant to the Parental Code may not be an auditor. The same applies to a person who is under a ban to engage in business (Chapter 9, section 10).

218. It is not enough that the auditor is competent. It is also necessary to see to it that he/she is independent of the company to be audited. The Companies Act – as well as the authorizing body, the Supervisory Board of Public Accountants (*Revisorsnämnden*) and the Institute for the Accountancy Profession in Sweden (*FAR*) – has tried to achieve this objective by prohibiting an accountant from acting as an auditor if he/she is not free from undue influence. Chapter 9, section 17, states that a person may not act as an auditor if he/she (1) owns shares in the company or another company within the same group; (2) is a director or the managing director of the company or of a subsidiary or assists the company in its book-keeping or the management of its assets or in the company's control thereof; (3) is employed by or otherwise subordinated to or dependent on the company or someone referred to in item 2; (4) is active in the same enterprise as someone who professionally assists the company in maintaining its books of original entry or managing its assets or in the company's control thereof; (5) is married to or co-habits with, or is a sibling or relative in directly ascending or descending relationship to a person specified in item 2; (6) is related by marriage to a person specified in item 2 in directly ascending or descending relationship or such that either is married to or sibling of the other; or (7) is indebted to the company or another company within the same group or has incurred an obligation for which the company has provided security.

With respect to companies where the demands for qualified auditing are highest (see paragraph 217 *supra*), the demands for independence are, with respect to item 4 *supra*, still higher (see Companies Act, Chapter 9, section 17, paragraph 2).

A person who is barred from being an auditor of the parent company may not be an auditor of a subsidiary company.

An auditor may not be assisted in his/her audit work by a person who may not act as an auditor. Where the company or the parent company has employees whose tasks are solely or primarily to perform internal audits, however, the auditor may be assisted by such employees in his/her audit work to an extent compatible with generally accepted auditing standards (Chapter 9, section 18).

219. It should be added that – in spite of all these rules – auditors are not always as independent as is desirable. Personal bonds may have developed over the years that the auditor has audited a company. Being the auditor of a well-known company with its shares on the stock exchange might be so prestigious that the auditor will be afraid of losing his/her job if he/she is 'too' efficient. And the management might have followed the advice of the auditor that later proves not to have been very wise. In addition, auditors sometimes have a tendency to take on too many appointments.

C. Expiry of Appointment

220. An appointment as auditor shall apply until the close of the general meeting that is held during the first financial year after the election of the auditor unless the articles of association state that the appointment shall last for a longer period (four years is the maximum). The same auditor may be reappointed – but in public companies with their shares on a regulated market the auditor must leave after seven years and cannot be re-elected for the next two years. (Chapter 9, sections 21 and 21 a.)

The appointment ceases anyhow at the request of the auditor – while the body that has appointed him/her is not allowed to remove the auditor unless there exists a just cause for such a removal (Chapter 9, section 22).

221. An auditor whose appointment expires prematurely is required by Chapter 9, section 23, of the Companies Act to notify the Companies Registration Office.

In his/her notification, he/she must report the observations he/she has made in the course of the audit he/she has carried out during the part of the current financial year covered by his/her appointment.

D. Duties

222. According to Chapter 9, section 3, of the Companies Act, the auditor(s) has (have) three main duties: (1) to examine the annual report: (2) to examine the accounts: and (3) to examine the administration of the company by the board of directors and the managing director. All these duties must be carried out according to generally accepted auditing standards. This means that the development of these standards has to be continuously taken into account.

223. The duties of the auditor(s) also include the submission of an auditor's report to the general meeting of shareholders for each financial year (Chapter 9, sections 5 and 28 et seq.). In this report, the auditor(s) is (are) required to supply the company with information about the result of his/her/their examination and to supply other interested parties with the information that they are, according to the Companies Act, entitled to. The shareholders need the information that the auditor's report contains when they shall pass resolutions with respect to the adoption of the income statement and the balance sheet, as well as, in some parents of a groups of enterprises, the adoption of the consolidated income statement and the consolidated balance sheet; allocation of the company's profit or loss according to the adopted balance sheet; and discharge (or non-discharge) from liability of the members of the board and the managing director. The Companies Act states that the report must – *inter alia* – include statements as to whether the annual report provides a true and fair representation of the company's results and financial position, whether the administration report is consistent with other parts of the annual report and whether the directors and the managing director should be discharged from liability towards the company. If an auditor in the course of his/her audit becomes aware of any acts or omissions by any director or the managing director that may give rise to liability, such fact shall be noted in the report. If the auditor has found that the company has not discharged its obligations with regard to different kinds of taxes, the auditor's report must also state this fact.

E. Minority Protection Rules

224. It should be added that Chapter 9 of the Companies Act, which covers auditing, includes special rules for the protection of the minority. First, if the owners of one-tenth of all shares or of one-third of the shares represented at the general meeting at which the election of auditors is to take place vote in favour of a proposal to add an extra auditor, to be appointed by the Company Registration Office, such an extra auditor must be appointed (section 9). Such an auditor has the same duties as those appointed by the majority. Second, an authorized public accountant or an approved public accountant who has passed a special examination must be appointed as auditor if the owners of one-tenth of all shares so request, even if such an auditor is not otherwise necessary in the company in question (section 16).

V. General and Special Examination

225. Earlier laymen could be appointed as auditors. When this possibility disappeared, a new chapter was added to the 1975 Companies Act with rules on general examination by laymen examiners. This chapter has found its place in the 2005 Companies Act as Chapter 10.

A person under age, in bankruptcy or with a custodian pursuant to the Parental Code may not be a general examiner. The same applies to a person who has been declared subject to an incapacity to engage in trade, Chapter 10, section 9.

The Act has tried to ensure that the examiner is independent by prescribing that any person is prohibited from acting as an examiner if he/she is not free from undue influence. Chapter 10, section 10, states therefore that a person is prohibited from acting as an examiner under the same conditions as accountants are prohibited from acting as auditors.

The task of a general examiner is to determine whether the company's operations have been conducted in an expedient and, from a financial perspective, satisfactory manner and whether the company's internal controls are sufficient. The examination shall be as detailed and extensive as required by customary praxis for this type of examination.

The general examiner shall at his/her examination comply with any instructions issued by the general meeting, provided that such do not contravene applicable law, the articles of association or customary practice. The intent of this rule is to have an examiner devote his/her control to the special purposes that a company with a special examiner probably has.

The examiner shall submit an examination report to the general meeting after each financial year. In this report, the examiner shall comment on those circumstances that are included in his/her general task and also on those circumstances that he/she was obliged to examine – see *supra*. Where the examiner finds cause to criticize any director or the managing director, the examiner shall state such in the report, together with information regarding the cause of the criticism.

226. The Companies Act has long contained rules on special examination. These rules originally found their place in the chapter on auditors, but were moved to their present location in connection with the legislation providing that only authorized public accountants and approved public accountants are to be accepted as auditors.

Where the owners of one-tenth of all shares or the owners of one-third of the shares represented at an annual general meeting, or a meeting called to discuss such a question, vote in favour of a proposal to appoint a special examiner, the county administrative board must appoint one or several examiners to carry out a special examination either of the administration and accounts of the company for a specific past period or of special measures or matters in relation to the company. This examination is of special character and is used mainly when the minority has reason to believe that something blameworthy has occurred in the company. Not only accountants, but also lawyers and other experts are appointed as special examiners.

VI. Worker Participation

227. Legislation on worker representation on the boards of directors of companies limited by shares was introduced in 1972. That legislation was of an experimental nature. In 1976, Sweden adopted permanent legislation, which was in turn replaced by the 1987 Act on Board Representation for Employees in the Private Sector. Although the Act states that its purpose is to guarantee employees insight into and influence over the activities of – among others – companies limited by shares, the right to appoint directors is not given to the employees as such, but to the unions that have concluded collective agreements with the company (provided there is such an union). This might be one of the reasons for the, relatively, high union membership that exists in Sweden (see paragraph 17 *supra*).

Not all companies, however, are under an obligation to open their boards to union-appointed directors. According to section 4 of the Act, it is only in companies with twenty-five or more employees that there exists a right for the union(s) to appoint directors: two directors and one deputy director for each director appointed. If, however, the company has activities in different branches of trade and industry and at least 1,000 employees, the union(s) has (have) the right to appoint three directors and one deputy director for each director. In a group of companies, the employees of all the enterprises of the group are counted, with a right for the union(s) to appoint directors in the parent company. The number of employee representatives on the board, however, may never exceed the number of directors appointed by other means.

The decision to make use of the right to appoint employee representatives is, according to section 6, made by a local trade union. If the decision concerns a parent company, it may be made by any local union within the group of companies. The board of directors of the company shall be notified of the decision made by the union.

The employee representatives are formally appointed by the local union(s) that is (are) bound by a collective agreement with the company or, in a group, with the enterprises in the group. If there are several such unions and the unions do not agree on how the representatives are to be elected, section 8 of the Act states in what order the different unions have the right to make the appointments.

Employee representatives 'should', according to section 9, be chosen from inside the company or, in the case of a parent company, from within the group of enterprises.

Normally, a union representative may not be a director of more than one company.

Under section 10, the maximum period of appointment of an employee representative is four years.

Union-appointed directors are normally bound by the same rules as other members of the board (section 11 of the Act). Some exceptions exist, however. Under section 12, for example, a deputy union director is given a mandatory right to attend and take part in discussions at board meetings, even if the regular director attends. Furthermore, one of the union directors has the right to participate in the work of a committee charged with preparing business that is later to be discussed at a board meeting (section 13). Finally, union directors are disqualified (on the grounds of bias) from participating in board discussions not only in the situations discussed in paragraph 199 *supra*, but also in those relating to collective agreements, industrial action (lockouts, strikes, etc.) or other matters where any trade union at the plant has a material interest that may be contrary to that of the company (section 14).

228. It is very common to have union representatives on the boards of Swedish companies limited by shares. The main problem associated with union representation seems to be keeping secret information secret in relation to the employees at the plant.

229. Special legislation regulates worker influence in the SE.

§4. Liquidation of the Company

I. Grounds for Winding-Up

A. Voluntary Winding-Up

230. The general meeting of shareholders may resolve that the company shall be wound up (Companies Act, Chapter 25, section 1). Such a decision is made by a simple (absolute) majority unless the articles of association require a qualified majority. Even if a qualified majority is required by the articles, the resolution may nevertheless be adopted by a simple majority if there is a ground for compulsory winding-up according to the Companies Act, Chapter 25, sections 11, 12 or 17.

When the general meeting has resolved that the company is to be wound up, the meeting must provide for the resolution to be reported to the Companies Registration Office, which appoints one or several liquidators. The liquidators replace the board of directors, and they are responsible for the liquidation of the company.

B. Compulsory Winding-Up

231. According to Chapter 25, sections 13–20, of the Companies Act, the company should be wound up if its equity is less than half of the registered share capital and its financial situation has not subsequently improved within the time specified in the Act in such a way that its equity amounts to the registered share capital.

Concerning the details of this rule, see paragraphs 88 et seq. *supra.*

232. Other grounds for compulsory winding-up are stated in the Companies Act, Chapter 25, sections 10 et seq. In some situations, the appropriate district court orders the winding-up of a company, while in other cases, the Companies Registration Office has the relevant authority.

233. A court of general jurisdiction shall decide upon liquidation – except in the situation when the court decides according to paragraph 231 *supra* – where the company is obliged to go into liquidation pursuant to its own articles of association, *or* where a shareholder, through abuse of his/her influence over the company, has intentionally participated in a violation of the Companies Act, the Annual Reports Act or the company's articles of association and the holders of one-tenth of all shares have made a petition to this effect (see further paragraph 235 *infra* on this alternative), *or, finally*, when the company's property has been surrendered for bankruptcy proceedings, after or in connection with such proceedings.

234. The Companies Registration Office shall (according to Chapter 25, section 11) decide that a company shall go into liquidation where:

(1) the company has failed to file in the prescribed manner the names of directors, managing director, special agent for service of process or auditor as shall be appointed pursuant to the Companies Act;
(2) the company has failed to file with the Companies Registration Office within eleven months from the end of its financial year the annual report and the auditor's report or, where applicable, group accounts and the auditor's report for the group;
(3) the company, having resolved that the share capital shall be determined in SEK instead of in EUR, has a share capital not amounting to SEK 50,000 and SEK 500,000, respectively (for private and public companies) and the company has failed to take the necessary measures; and
(4) the company has failed to fulfil its divestment obligation after having acquired its own shares without having taken the steps prescribed in the Companies Act.

An order for the winding-up of the company will not be made, however, if the actual ground ceases to exist while the matter is pending at the Companies Registration Office and the fees that have been charged with respect to the costs in the proceeding have been paid.

235. As to the question of abuse mentioned in paragraph 233 *supra*, the following information should be added.

One of the main problems in Swedish company law is affording the minority suitable protection without making the form of a company unsuited to commercial activities. The protection that is afforded to the minority in Swedish companies is in reality fairly weak, but there is one ultimate safeguard for the minority in the form of a right to demand that the company be wound up or, if this would be too harmful to other interests, to have its shares redeemed. Therefore, the Companies Act states, in Chapter 25, sections 21–23, that where a shareholder has intentionally abused his/her influence in the company by taking part in a violation of the Companies Act, the Annual Reports Act or the articles of association, the court may, at the request of the owners of one-tenth of all shares, declare that the company is to be wound up. This sanction, however, may be used only if there is special cause for doing so in view of the duration of the abuse or if there are other special reasons. It is not intended that this ground should be readily invoked; it is in fact the final recourse that the Act offers to shareholders who have suffered serious detriment. But, as indicated above, the court has the option to order, at the request of the company, that the company redeem the plaintiff's shares within a specified period of time, instead of declaring that the company shall be wound up. When considering this question, the court is required to pay special attention to the interests of employees and creditors. However, under no circumstances may redemption take place where it would result in the equity of the company being less than half of the share capital. (The Act provides additional rules on the valuation of assets in the balance sheet in this situation.) Should the company fail to redeem the shares as ordered within the specified period, the court must, at the request of the plaintiff, declare that the company shall be wound up.

236. If a court or the registration authority orders the winding-up of a company, it must simultaneously appoint one or more liquidators. The liquidators replace the board of directors and are responsible for carrying out the liquidation of the company.

C. Other Grounds

237. Besides what has already been said on the grounds for winding-up companies, it should be mentioned that a company can also cease to exist as the result of a bankruptcy proceeding. If the bankruptcy is terminated without a surplus, the company is dissolved when the bankruptcy is terminated. If there is a surplus, on the other hand, there is a ground for winding-up of the company (see Chapter 25, section 51).

II. The Liquidation Process

238. The provisions of the Companies Act on the board of directors and individual directors are also applicable to liquidators unless specifically provided otherwise.

The auditors and the general and special examiners of the company are not replaced, and their duties are the same as before the liquidation process began. The auditors are, however, under the obligation to state in their report(s) whether in their opinion the liquidation is being unnecessarily delayed. General meetings, finally, are held according to the same rules as discussed above unless otherwise provided for in Chapter 25 on the liquidation of companies.

239. As soon as the company has entered into liquidation, the resigning board of directors and managing director have to submit a report on their management of the affairs of the company for the period for which no report has previously been presented at a general meeting. If the period in question also covers the preceding financial year, a separate report shall be presented for that year, including, in the case of a parent company that is obliged to prepare group accounts, consolidated accounts.

240. The first task of the liquidators is to summon the unknown creditors of the company (Chapter 25, section 34). This is done at the Companies Registration Office. Together with their application, the liquidators submit a list of the known creditors of the company, and the Office notifies those creditors that are listed of the liquidation. The Office then summons the unknown creditors to state their claims at the Registration Office. A creditor who is not included in the list of known creditors and who does not state his/her claim by the specified date loses his/her right to payment for his/her claim unless he/she can show that the debtor knew about it before the date specified in the notice.

Under Chapter 25, section 35, of the Companies Act, the liquidators must as soon as possible, by public auction or in other appropriate ways, convert the company's property into cash to the extent that this is necessary for its liquidation. They must also pay the debts of the company. The activities of the company may be continued to the degree necessary to expedite the liquidation process and to give employees a reasonable time to find new employment.

For each financial year that the liquidation continues, the liquidators have to submit an annual report (Chapter 25, section 37).

When the date for stating claims set forth in the summons to unknown creditors has expired and all known debts have been paid, the liquidators are to distribute the remaining assets to the shareholders. If a debt is disputed, or is not due for payment, or cannot be paid for other reasons, adequate funds must be reserved for its payment, and only the remainder is distributed (Chapter 25, section 38).

241. A shareholder who wishes to challenge the distribution must, under the Companies Act, Chapter 25, section 39, bring an action against the company not later than three months after the final distribution was presented at a general meeting of shareholders.

242. When the liquidators have completed their task, they must as soon as possible submit a final account of their administration in the form of an administration report concerning the liquidation in its entirety. This report must also contain particulars of the distribution of surplus assets. Accounts for the entire liquidation period are to be attached to the report. The report and the accounts are to be delivered to the auditors. Within one month, the auditors must submit a report on the final accounts and the administration of the company during its liquidation. The liquidators then convene a general meeting for the purpose of examining the final accounts. At that meeting, a resolution shall be passed with respect to discharge from liability for the liquidators (Chapter 25, section 40).

243. When the liquidators have submitted the final accounts to the general meeting, the company is dissolved. This must immediately be reported to the Companies Registration Office for registration purposes. In spite of the fact that the company is dissolved, a general meeting is to be called to consider whether an action for damages is to be brought if the liquidators were not discharged from liability at the final general meeting (Chapter 25, section 43).

244. If during the liquidation process the liquidators find that the company has become insolvent and cannot pay the costs of liquidation, they will have the company declared bankrupt.

245. Liquidation must be resumed, even if the company is dissolved, if it appears that it has further assets, or if an action is brought against it, or if for some other reason a liquidation measure is needed.

246. When the decision to have a company wound up is made by the general meeting or by the court, the general meeting may decide that the liquidation process is to cease and that the activities of the company are to be resumed, provided that: (1) there is no ground for winding-up the company in accordance with the Companies Act, Chapter 25, section 11 or 12 (i.e., where the situation is that dealt with in paragraph 234 or where the company is obliged to go into liquidation pursuant to its own articles of association); (2) the company has been subject to proceedings according to paragraph 231 *supra*, but the equity of the company now amounts to the registered share capital; and (3) no distribution of assets has taken place. Concerning the details, see the Companies Act, Chapter 25, section 45.

§5. MERGERS, COMPULSORY REDEMPTION OF MINORITY SHARES AND DE-MERGERS

I. Mergers

247. A merger (*fusion* in Swedish) means that the assets and liabilities of one or more companies pass to an acquiring company without any liquidation of the disappearing company(ies). Upon a merger, the owners of the disappearing company(ies) receive payment for their shares in the form of either shares in the acquiring company or shares and money.

248. Rules on merger are found in Chapter 23 of the Companies Act. This chapter was revised in 1994 with the aim of bringing the Swedish legislation into conformity with the European Economic Community (EEC) Directive of 1978 concerning mergers of public limited liability companies. The Swedish rules are mainly – but not in every detail – the same for private and public companies.

A merger may take place only where the transferor and the transferee companies have the same accounting currency (Chapter 23, section 3).

249. The Companies Act contains rules on two kinds of merger: (1) merger through either the absorption of a company that is not wholly owned by the absorbing company or the combination of two or more companies into a new company formed specially for that purpose and (2) merger through the absorption by a parent company of a subsidiary in which it owns 100% of the shares. I will start with alternative (1).

250. The boards of the companies to be merged have to draw up a common plan for the merger (Chapter 23, section 6). This plan must contain information of importance for the merger (Chapter 23, sections 7–10). It must be scrutinized by the auditors of the merging companies or other qualified auditors. Their report is added to the plan (Chapter 23, section 11). The plan is usually to be registered at the registration authority, and an announcement of what it contains or where it can be inspected is published in the Official Gazette (Chapter 23, section 14). When this has been done, the plan is presented to the shareholders of the disappearing company(ies), who have to decide at a general meeting whether or not it is to be approved. A minority of 5% of the owners of all the shares of the acquiring company have the right to demand that the same plan also be put on the agenda of a general meeting of that company (Chapter 23, section 15). At the general meeting(s), a qualified majority of two-thirds both of the votes cast and of the shares represented at the meeting is required for the plan to be adopted. However, if the disappearing company is a public company and the acquiring company is a private company, the decision needs the approval of all the shareholders present at the meeting, with the further stipulation that these shareholders must represent nine-tenths of the shares of the disappearing company. The rule is the same when the disappearing company is a public company whose shares are traded on a regulated market and the merger consideration includes shares that are not traded on such a market (Chapter 23, section 17).

Not only the shareholders are affected by a merger, however. So, too, are the holders of special rights in the disappearing company(ies) – such as the holders of convertible instruments. The Companies Act (Chapter 23, section 5) states that such holders must be given at least the same rights in the acquiring company as they had in the disappearing one unless, under the merger plan, they are paid in cash.

Creditors are another category for which a merger is of great importance.

For the creditors of the disappearing company, the merger means in reality that they now have a claim on a new debtor, but a merger can also mean a weaker position for the debtors of an acquiring company. The Companies Act therefore prescribes that all known creditors of the disappearing company are to be informed when the plan for the merger has been approved and that the same applies to the creditors of the acquiring company unless the auditors have stated in their report that the status of those creditors will not be endangered by the merger (Chapter 23, section 19).

251. The acquiring company or, in the case of a combination, the oldest of the acquiring companies now makes an application to the Companies Registration Office for permission to take the steps foreseen in the merger plan (Chapter 23, section 20). The Office checks whether there is any legal bar to the merger and, if no such bar exists, notifies the creditors of the disappearing company(ies). If the auditors have stated that the merger might endanger the creditors of the acquiring company, they, too, are notified (Chapter 23, sections 22 and 23). If any creditor contests the application, the procedure is transferred to the appropriate district court, which will grant the application if the contesting creditor receives payment in full or satisfactory security for his/her claim (Chapter 23, section 24).

The board of the acquiring company notifies the registration authority in order to register the merger (Chapter 23, section 25). When registration has been effected, the disappearing company(ies) is (are) dissolved. Its (their) assets and debts are in principle transferred to the acquiring company at the same time, and the shareholders of the disappearing company(ies) become shareholders of the acquiring company (Chapter 23, section 26).

252. When a wholly owned subsidiary is merged with a parent company, the decision to merge can normally be made by the boards of directors of these two companies. But a minority that owns 5% of the shares of the parent company has the right to demand that the decision be made by its general meeting. The creditors of the two companies are to be notified under the same conditions and in the same way as they are with other mergers (Chapter 23, section 32).

253. Since 15 February 2008, the Companies Act has contained rules on cross-border mergers.

254. Finally, competition law and labour law are implicated with regard to mergers. With respect to competition legislation, the Companies Act refers to bars under both the Competition Act and the European Council Regulation (EC) Number. 139/2004 of 20 January 2004 on the control of concentration between undertakings. Concerning labour law, reference should be made to the 1976 Act on Codetermination in Working Life.

II. Compulsory Redemption of Minority Shares

255. It appears from what has been said that a merger by the absorption of a wholly owned subsidiary is a fairly uncomplicated matter. The Companies Act even facilitates the acquisition of the remaining shares of a subsidiary when a parent company is such a dominant owner that most of the Act's rules for the protection of the minority are no longer able to prevent abuses – that is, when the minority has less than 10% of the shares. Such acquisition is also seen as a means of facilitating an often-necessary restructuring of Swedish company structure in order to form strong and efficient enterprises. Consequently, when a parent company alone or together with one or more of its subsidiaries owns more than nine-tenths of the shares in a company, the parent company is entitled to redeem the remaining shares from the other shareholders of the subsidiary (Chapter 22, section 1).

As I have said, the rules of the Companies Act aimed at protecting the minority are based to a large extent on the holding of 10% of the shares, and the rule just mentioned is reciprocal: Any person who owns shares that may be redeemed has the right to demand that his/her shares be redeemed by the parent company.

Redemption of shares at the request of parent companies is very common in Sweden; situations where a single shareholder or a minority of shareholders requests the redemption, on the other hand, are very unusual.

256. Any dispute over whether a redemption right or obligation exists or over the redemption price is to be submitted to three arbitrators. The arbitrator to be chosen by the minority shareholders is usually appointed by a legal representative of these shareholders who is appointed by the Stockholm District Court. With a few exceptions, the arbitration procedure follows Swedish arbitration law; for details, see the 1999 Arbitration Act. Some exceptions exist, however: The parent company has to pay all the costs of the arbitration procedure – including the costs for the legal representative representing the minority shareholders – unless, for special reasons, the arbitrators declare another shareholder liable for these costs, wholly or partly. Further, a party who is not satisfied with the award is entitled to bring an action before the court within sixty days of being served with notice of the award. These deviations from normally applicable arbitration law are due to the very special situation existing in a redemption case.

The question of whether or not the conditions for redemption are met is usually not difficult to answer. It is more difficult, on the other hand, to decide the price to be paid by the redeeming company for the shares in the subsidiary. To facilitate this procedure, the Companies Act states (Chapter 2, section 2) that the purchase price for a share shall be determined in such manner that it corresponds to the price for the share that might be expected upon a sale under normal circumstances. With respect to a share that is traded on a regulated market or an equivalent market outside the EEA, the purchase price shall correspond to the listed value unless special grounds dictate otherwise. The purchase price shall be determined taking into consideration the circumstances prevailing at the time a request for arbitration was made; if special reasons exist, the amount may, however, be determined taking into consideration the circumstances prevailing at an earlier time. Where, finally, a demand for a buyout of shares pursuant to Chapter 22 of the Companies Act was preceded by a public offer to acquire all shares not already held by the offeror and such offer was accepted by the holders of more than nine-tenths of the shares to which the offer relates, the purchase price shall correspond to the consideration offered unless special cause dictates otherwise. Special grounds for a different price might be, for example, that a substantial period has elapsed since the offer was made or that the information given in conjunction with the offer was not sufficient.

To enable the redeeming company to obtain the shares at an early stage, the arbitrators (or, if the dispute has gone that far, the court) may declare that the shareholders are obliged to transfer their shares although the redemption price has not yet been decided. This rule, which is stated in the Companies Act, Chapter 22, section 12, is of great importance to the parent company because of the minority protection rules that do not depend on a certain number of shares (such as the obligation of the general meeting and the board of directors and the managing director to see to it that the general clauses of the Companies Act – see paragraph 48 *supra* – are not infringed). An award obliging the shareholders to transfer their shares may be made only if the right or obligation of redemption is not disputed by any of the parties or if it is otherwise clear that such a right or obligation exists, the majority shareholder has provided security for the future purchase price and interest and the security has been approved by the arbitrators or the court.

257. When security has been furnished and otherwise when a duly determined redemption price has been paid, the parent company becomes the owner of the redeemed shares.

III. De-mergers

258. Swedish companies legislation has contained rules on mergers since 1948, but it did not contain any rules on de-mergers until the 2005 Companies Act was promulgated.

259. One way to split a company is to transfer its assets and liabilities to two or several other companies and make the transferring company disappear without any liquidation, as though taken over by the other company(ies). Another way to split up a company is to transfer part of its assets and liabilities to another company. In this situation, the transferring company will remain but with less assets than before. Both these alternatives are possible according to the 2005 Companies Act, Chapter 24, section 1.

All companies involved in a de-merger transaction must have the same accounting currency (Chapter 24, section 3).

The rules on de-mergers are mainly the same for private and public companies.

260. The assets of the transferring company will diminish through the de-merger. Its shareholders should consequently be compensated through de-merger consideration. Such consideration can consist of shares in the transferee company or of a combination of shares and cash. More than half of the consideration shall, however, consist of shares (Chapter 24, section 2). It may never consist of promissory notes or other property.

The rules in the Companies Act aimed at the protection of creditors and other third parties in connection with the formation of a company could be disregarded during a de-merger procedure. Therefore, the Companies Act states that the company(ies) that is(are) going to be formed must have net proceeds of at least the same size as the share capital of the new company(ies). The de-merger plan prepared by the boards of the companies involved in the de-merger procedure is nevertheless used as the basic document instead of the memorandum of association, which is used at a regular formation of a company.

261. The boards of the companies involved in the de-merger procedure have to draw up a common plan for the de-merger (Chapter 24, section 7). This plan shall contain information of importance for the de-merger (Chapter 24, sections 8–12). It must be scrutinized by qualified auditors in all participating companies. Their report is added to the plan (Chapter 24, section 13). The plan is to be registered at the registration authority, and an announcement of what it contains or where it can be inspected is published in the Official Gazette (Chapter 24, section 16). When this has been done, the plan is presented to the shareholders of the transferring company(ies), who have to decide at a general meeting whether or not it is to be approved. A minority of 5% of the owners of all the shares of the acquiring company(ies) has the right to demand that the same plan also be put on the agenda of a general meeting of that(these) company(ies) (Chapter 24, section 17). At the general meeting(s), a qualified majority of two-thirds both of the votes cast and of the shares represented at the meeting is required for the plan to be adopted. If there are several classes of shares in the companies, such majority must be achieved in each class (Chapter 24, section 19). In some situations, the majority requirement is still higher. When the plan has been approved by the shareholders, the transferring company should turn to the Companies Registration Office and ask for its permission to continue. The Registration Office has to determine whether the situation of the creditors of the participating companies could become endangered through the de-merger. If the Registration Office finds that this is the case, the de-merger procedure may not continue unless the creditors receive full payment or satisfactory security for their claims (Chapter 24, section 26). When authorization to implement the de-merger plan has been given, the de-merger is registered and completed.

Where only private companies are concerned, a simplified procedure can be used if all shareholders have signed the de-merger plan.

262. The de-merger plan shall state which company is liable for the debts of the transferring company(ies) after the de-merger. That company is liable without any limitation. However, if it cannot pay its debts, the other companies to which property has been transferred are liable together with the first company – but only up to the amount that they have received in connection with the de-merger (Chapter 24, section 19).

Not only the shareholders are affected by a de-merger, however. So, too, are the holders of special rights in the transferring company – such as the holders of convertible instruments. The Companies Act (Chapter 24, section 6) states that such holders must be given at least the same rights in the acquiring company as they had in the transferring one unless, under the de-merger plan, they are paid.

§6. Companies with Special Limitations on Dividends

263. The last chapter in the 2005 Companies Act concerns companies that may not, according to their articles of association, distribute more than a limited dividend to their shareholders. The idea behind this regulation is that such private companies could be an alternative in areas where public money is involved – such as health care and housing.

264. The limitation is shown by three letters added to the business name of the company: *svb* (an abbreviation for *Särskild vinstutdelnings begränsning* – that is, special limitation on dividends) if it is does not follow already from the name of the company that it has this special character (Chapter 32, section 17).

In a company with special limitations on dividends, in addition to the provisions of the Companies Act in Chapter 17, sections 3 and 4 (the prudence rule; see paragraph 71 *supra*), the following shall apply concerning value transfers from the company: Such transfers may not, during one financial year, exceed the government borrowing rate (*statslåneräntan*) plus 1% point on the capital that the shareholders have contributed to the company as payment for shares. However, to this amount may be added an amount that has been available for value transfers at the annual general meeting during each of the preceding five financial years, less any value transfers that have occurred during that same period (Chapter 32, section 5).

A company with special limitations on dividends that is included in a group may not, other than in the cases stated in the previous paragraph, transfer funds to another company in the group in such a way that the transferred amount would exceed the limitation (Chapter 32, section 8).

The auditor of the company shall determine that the company has not violated the stated limitation. If such a violation has occurred, the auditor is obliged to report this fact in his/her auditor's report, which he/she must also send to the Companies Registration Office (Chapter 32, section 3).

In a company with special limitations on dividends, a resolution may not be adopted that the company shall no longer be a company with special limitations on dividends (Chapter 32, section 15).

If, in an svb-company, the provisions on special limitations on dividends have been disregarded, both repayment and, if repayment cannot be effected, deficiency payment might be claimed. Further, the appropriate district court will order the winding-up of the company if it has disregarded what the Companies Act contains concerning limitation on dividend and adjustment has not occurred (Chapter 32, section 13).

When an svb-company is wound up, the shareholders may receive what they have paid for their shares and also what they may receive as dividend (see *supra*). What exceeds this amount shall inure to the other company(ies) with special limitations on dividends as stated in the articles of association. If these articles do not contain any such provisions, the assets shall inure to the State Inheritance Fund (*Allmänna arvsfonden*) (Chapter 32, section 14).

§7. Groups of Companies

I. Background

265. A group of enterprises (*koncern* in Swedish) consists of a number of legally independent enterprises of which one, the parent, dominates the others. Rules on groups are in Sweden found both in the Companies Act and in other legislation, such as the 1995 Annual Reports Act. The rules on groups were first brought into company law by the 1944 Companies Act.

266. Rules on groups of enterprises have been found to be necessary because of the possibility that those managing the parent will make decisions about the business transactions of the dominated enterprises in such a way that the rules to protect the equity of the individual enterprises are set aside. This was demonstrated in Sweden in the early 1930s by a well-known financial failure, the *Kreuger crash*, which was in fact one of the starting points for the improvement of company legislation that resulted in the 1944 Companies Act.

II. Definition

267. A group of enterprises is defined in Chapter 1, section 11, of the 2005 Companies Act as a parent company and its subsidiaries. A parent company and a subsidiary are in turn defined in one of four ways. A company is a parent company and another legal person is a subsidiary where the company (1) holds more than one-half of the voting rights of all shares or interests in the legal person; (2) owns shares or interests in the legal person and, as a consequence of an agreement with other owners of such legal person, controls more than one-half of the voting rights of all shares or interests in the legal person; (3) owns shares or interests in the legal person and is entitled to appoint or remove more than one-half of the members of its board of directors or equivalent management body; or (4) owns shares or interests in the legal person and is entitled to exercise a sole controlling influence there-over as a consequence of an agreement with the legal person or as a consequence of provisions of the legal person's articles of association, partnership agreement or comparable statutes. This definition presupposes that the parent company is a Swedish company, while the subsidiaries are included whether or not they are Swedish. (Indirect group relationships are equalized with direct group relationships.)

III. Special Rules on Groups

268. The Annual Reports Act requires – with certain exceptions stated in that Act in Chapter 7, sections 2, 3 and 3 a – that a parent company prepare and make public, in addition to its own annual report, consolidated accounts consisting of a consolidated income statement, a consolidated balance sheet, notes, a directors' report and a funds statement (Chapter 7, sections 1–4). These accounts shall reflect the same date as the parent company's balance sheet. The intent of this legislation is to ensure that shareholders, creditors, employees and others are given information concerning the real financial situation of both the group and the individual enterprises making up the group.

269. The fact that a company is the parent of a group is of importance also from a company law perspective. The maximum that may be paid as dividends to the shareholders is what is stated in the balance sheet as the company's or, in case of a group, the group's non-restricted equity. As stated in the Companies Act, Chapter 17, section 3, a value transfer may not take place where, after the transfer, there is insufficient coverage for the company's restricted equity; further, where the company is a parent company, consideration shall also be given to the demands with respect to the group's equity, which are imposed by the nature, scope and risks associated with the group's operations, as well as the group's need to strengthen its balance sheet, liquidity and financial position in general.

270. Other relevant provisions in the Companies Act include the following. A subsidiary may not – with some exceptions stated in the Act – accept shares in its parent company as security (Chapter 19, section 3), nor may a subsidiary – with certain exceptions also stated in the Act – acquire shares in its parent company

(Chapter 19, section 7). Board members and managing directors shall, upon assuming office, notify the company of their holdings of shares in the company and in other companies within the same group unless such has taken place prior thereto; they shall also notify the company of subsequent changes in these shareholdings within one month (Chapter 8, section 45). The board members and the managing director have a duty to provide information at general meetings not only on circumstances that apply to the company itself, but also on different circumstances that apply to the company's relationship to other group companies, and, where the company is the parent of a group, they have the duty to provide information on the group's accounts and certain other circumstances regarding subsidiaries (Chapter 7, section 32). A person who is not authorized to serve as an auditor of a parent company may also not serve as an auditor of its subsidiary (Chapter 9, section 17). At least one of the auditors of a subsidiary should also be an auditor of the parent company (Chapter 9, section 20). The prohibition against loans from the company to shareholders includes persons owing shares or holding positions within the same group (Chapter 21, section 1). As for the importance of the existence of a group of companies in connection with a merger involving a redemption of shares in a subsidiary, compare paragraph 255 *supra*. Finally, when a parent company alone or together with one or more of its subsidiaries owns more than nine-tenths of the shares in a company, the parent company is entitled to redeem the remaining shares from the other shareholders of the subsidiary (Chapter 22, section 1).

271. As mentioned in paragraph 227 *supra*, the right of the trade unions to elect directors comes into effect with regard to the parent of a group of companies when there are a mere twenty-five employees in the group.

Finally, it should be mentioned that the Companies Act does not contain any rules on lifting the corporate veil. There are nevertheless some reported cases where Swedish courts have lifted the corporate veil, and one condition that could be of importance in this connection is whether there is a parent–subsidiary relationship.

§8. Taxation of Companies and Shareholders

272. Under Swedish tax law, both the company as such and the shareholders have to pay taxes on their respective incomes. Tax law as applied to companies is consequently built on double taxation.

Swedish law on company taxation is based on the idea that profits that are not consumed by the owner(s) should be favourably taxed in order to facilitate investment and company expansion. The nominal tax on the profits of a company is 22%.

There has long been a close connection between the accounts of a company and its taxation. Taxation is thus still often based on the result entered in the accounts, which is arrived at by applying generally accepted accounting principles. This connection between accounts and taxation has, however, ceased to apply to small, private companies.

All operating costs are in principle deductible.

The basis for the computation of tax is the profit before tax. However, another deduction should also be mentioned in this connection, and that is the right in principle to use a deficit from one financial year when the company once again shows a positive result – that is, the right to carry forward. There is no time limit on making such a deduction, but a deduction cannot be postponed when there are profits against which it can be offset. In case of a transfer of ownership there is, however, a limit as to what may be carried forward.

With regard to profit paid by the company to its non-corporate shareholders, the capital income tax is 30% on dividends. To achieve a kind of neutrality between insiders of close companies and other taxpayers in Swedish society, however, the tax law states that if a company is in reality dominated by one or a small number of natural persons, and the dominant owner is active either alone or together with another person, and the company pays dividends to him/her that exceed a certain percentage based on his/her contribution of capital to the company, then the excess dividend is treated as income from employment and therefore might – depending on the income of the person in question – be taxed at as high a rate as approximately 56%–57%.

It should be added that Swedish tax legislation contains a number of rules aimed at preventing companies from giving managers, co-owners and relatives of owners of close companies special privileges. These rules concern, for example, sales to or purchases from the company, the purchase by the company of property that is not normally connected with the kind of business in which it is engaged, loans to and from the company (including those that are not allowed under company law; see paragraph 75 *supra*) and the interest on such loans and the leasing of premises for the company.

A group of companies is not accepted in Swedish tax law as a legal entity of its own. Tax legislation is based on the definition from private law discussed above (see paragraph 267 *supra*), but sometimes the rules of private law are not used – as is the case, for example, with contributions made inside the group with the aim of levelling profits within the group. Tax law also contains certain rules aimed at facilitating the use of company groups, such as the right to make tax-deductible contributions to companies inside the group, and on companies whose operations are carried out on behalf of another company under a special agreement (*kommissionärsbolag*).

The tax legislation contains a set of rules designed to prevent the adverse consequences of chain taxation (i.e., when the shares of one company are owned by another company).

It should finally be added that what is said in this paragraph on taxation is based on the situation in December 2014 and that taxation is an area where legislation is very often amended.

Chapter 2. Private Vis-à-Vis Public Companies

273. As noted in the Introduction, there are two kinds of ordinary share companies in Sweden, private and public companies. The same Companies Act covers both kinds. When the rules are different for private and public companies, the Act usually starts with the rule for private companies. When the rule for public companies is different, the relevant section usually contains a reference to the section in the same chapter that states the rule for public companies. Often the rules that are applicable to public companies are brought together in the final part of the relevant chapter. When the public companies are covered by supplementary rules, the systems vary: These supplementing rules are sometimes brought together in the end of the relevant chapter, but sometimes they are to be found in their systematic context.

There will now follow an overview of what the Companies Act contains on special rules for private and public companies.

§1. General Rules and Rules Concerning the Formation of a Company

274. The Companies Act contains a chapter on companies with special limitations on dividends (see paragraph 263 *supra*). Such companies must be private companies (Chapter 1, section 4). The minimum share capital of a private company is SEK 50,000 (Chapter 1, section 5) and of a public company SEK 500,000 (Chapter 1, section 14) or, in both cases, the equivalent amount in EUR. Companies with special limitations on dividends excepted, only public companies and their shareholders may turn to the public to obtain financial resources. Shares or subscription rights in private companies and debentures or warrants issued by private companies may not be sold in an organized marketplace (Chapter 1, section 7). The memorandum of association of a private company does not have to state the costs for the preparation of the memorandum of association and similar work, even if these costs are to be paid by the company, while the memorandum of association of a public company shall contain information regarding all costs associated with the formation that the company is to pay. The Companies Act contains rules on deferred non-cash consideration in public – but not in private – companies. (To the name of a public company must be added the letters (*publ*) unless the name itself contains the word *publikt*.)

§2. Split or Reverse Split

275. The shareholders' consent is needed when the shares are not traded on a regulated market (Chapter 4, section 47).

§3. SHAREHOLDERS' MEETING

276. The articles of association of a private company may state that the notice to attend a general meeting shall be issued two weeks in advance, while the minimum time in a public company is four weeks.

A public company with its shares on a regulated market must provide its shareholders with a proxy form to be used by those who wish to do so (Chapter 7, section 54a). A resolution stating that a person who is not a shareholder shall be entitled to be present at a general meeting of a public company, if the resolution is adopted with simple majority (Chapter 7, section 55.) In a private company, however, such a resolution is valid only where it is supported by all shareholders present at the general meeting (Chapter 7, section 6).

The right of the shareholders to demand information from the board and the managing director is limited in a public company, as compared with a private company – except at the annual general meeting. In fact, the rules concerning the convening of a general meeting are stricter in public than in private companies. For instance shall elections be held through open voting. (However, a ballot shall in a private company be held where so requested by any person entitled to vote, while in public companies, voting shall take place by ballot only where the general meeting resolves thereon, see Chapter 7, sections 39 and 58.) And with respect to resolutions to remove a member from the board of directors appointed by the general meeting, the articles of association of a public company may not contain a provision that such a removal requires more than simple majority.

If the articles of association state that a dispute between the company and the board of directors, a member of the board, the managing director, a liquidator or a shareholder shall be determined by arbitration proceedings, the company is usually responsible for the compensation to the arbitrators where the company is a public company (Chapter 7, section 60).

Furthermore, for public companies registered with a regulated market, the Companies Act contains certain rules that should be applied at a general meeting. Such a company must, in its notice, give information concerning the total number of shares and votes in the company, as well as information about how many of these shares that are owned by the company itself (Chapter 7, section 63). The company may also, under certain conditions use electronic devices for conveying information to its shareholders (Chapter 7, section 64 et seq.). The annual general meeting must also decide on guidelines for the remuneration to the top executives of the company (Chapter 7, section 61).

§4. MANAGEMENT

277. The number of directors may in a private company be one or two, provided that there is at least one deputy director (Chapter 8, section 1). However, in a public company, the board of directors shall comprise not less than three members (Chapter 8, section 46). The board of directors shall be appointed by the general meeting unless the articles of association provide that one or more members of the board shall be appointed in another manner. However, in a public company, more than one-half of the members of the board must be appointed by the general meeting (Chapter 8, section 47).

Chapter 8 of the Companies Act contains quit a few rules that only are applicable on public companies. Among others the following: Prior to a board election, the chairman of the board of directors shall provide the general meeting with information regarding the positions in other enterprises held by the person to whom the election relates (section 48). The person elected as chairman of the board of directors may not be the managing director of the company (section 49). In a private company, a managing director may be appointed; in a public company, a managing director shall be appointed. Furthermore, if the In public company has is registered at a regularly market, the board must nominate an auditing committee unless the board can itself monitor the duties that such a committee has to carry out.

§5. Audits

277.1. Small-sized private companies may refrain from having any auditor (Chapter 9, section 1).

278. In a public company with its shares on a regulated market, at least one of the auditors shall be an authorized public accountant (Chapter 9, section 13).

In a public company with its shares on a regulated market an auditor cannot hold office for more than seven years (Chapter 9, section 21a).

§6. Capital Contribution

279. The rules concerning information provided to the shareholders on bonus issues are sometimes somewhat different in public companies compared with the rules in private companies. (For a company with its shares on a regulated market, the subscription price may be lower than the quotient values of the earlier shares, provided that an amount corresponding to the difference between the subscription price and the quotient value of the shares is transferred to the share capital through a transfer from the company's shareholders' equity in general or through a write-up of the value of listed assets.) Where the new shares, the warrants or the convertible instruments are to be listed on a regulated market, a resolution to issue such shares, warrants or convertible instruments may contain an authorization for the board of directors or a person appointed by the board from among its members to determine, prior to the commencement of the subscription period, the amount to be paid for each share, warrant or convertible instrument and also some of the conditions for the issue. (Rights of setoff are more common in public than in private companies in relation to both new issues and issues of warrants and of convertible instruments.) Payment in cash for new shares or convertible instruments shall in a private company take place through a deposit in a bank account opened by the company for this purpose. In a public company, payment may also be made directly to the company. (Chapter 16 of the Companies Act contains special provisions regarding public companies and subsidiaries of such companies in the areas of (a) new issues and issues of warrants and convertible instruments; (b) the transfer of shares, warrants or convertible instruments issued by a company within a group of companies; and (c) certain kinds of loans. According to these rules, any decision to issue new shares, warrants or convertible instruments to the directors of the board, the managing director, other employees or close relatives of these persons or to legal persons over which such natural persons have a controlling influence must be taken by the general meeting and with a majority of at least nine-tenths both of the votes and of the shares represented at the meeting. Information concerning such issues and transfers must also be furnished in the directors' report.)

§7. Capital Protection

280. The Companies Act has long contained rules forbidding – in principle – the acquisition of a company's own shares. This rule is still in force in private companies. However, a public company with its shares on a regulated market is allowed to acquire its own shares to the extent that the company's holding of its own shares following the acquisition would not exceed one-tenth of all shares in the company (Chapter 19, sections 13–15). Shares in the company held by any subsidiary shall be deemed to be shares held by the company.

A proposal that the share capital shall be reduced for repayment to the shareholders through the retirement of shares (a buyout) may, where the shares are listed on a regulated market, contain an authorization for the board of directors or a person appointed by the board from among its members to determine, prior to the commencement of the buyout, the amount by which the share capital shall be reduced and the amount to be paid for each bought-out share (Chapter 20, section 37).

Loans from a company to its shareholders, etc. are to a large degree prohibited. Exemptions from these prohibitions may, however, be granted except in relation to public companies, where exemptions may not be granted with respect to the provision of an advance or loan or security in order to acquire shares in the company (Chapter 21, section 12).

§8. Buyout of Minority Shareholder

281. The buyout price shall usually be determined in such a manner that it corresponds to the price for the share that might be expected upon a sale under normal circumstances. With respect to shares that are traded on a regulated market, the purchase price shall, however, correspond to the list value unless special grounds dictate otherwise. (Notices to minority shareholders are somewhat different in public and in private companies.)

§9. Merger and De-merger

282. The rules on mergers are mainly the same for private and public companies. The time for the submission of the merger plan to the general meetings of the transferor companies is, however, somewhat shorter when only private companies are concerned. And the procedure is simpler when all concerned companies are private companies and all their shareholders have signed the merger plan. (Where any of the transferor companies is a public company and the transferee company is a private company, the decision of the public company regarding approval of the merger plan shall be valid only where it is supported by all shareholders present at the general meeting and where such shareholders together represent not less than nine-tenths of all shares of the company.) The rules on de-mergers are mainly the same for private and public companies. The time for the submission of the de-merger plan to the general meetings of the different companies is, however, somewhat shorter when only private companies are concerned. And the procedure is simpler when all concerned companies are private companies and all their shareholders have signed the de-merger plan. (Where the transferor company is a public company and any of the transferee companies is a private company, the decision of the public company regarding approval of the de-merger plan shall be valid only where it is supported by all shareholders present at the general meeting and where these shareholders together represent not less than nine-tenths of all shares of the company.)

§10. Miscellaneous

283. A resolution that a private company shall become a public company shall be adopted by the general meeting with an absolute (simple) majority (Chapter 26, section 1). A resolution that a public company shall become a private company is, on the other hand, valid only where it is supported by all shareholders present at the general meeting and where these shareholders together represent not less than nine-tenths of all shares of the company (Chapter 26, section 6).

Chapter 3. Companies with Special Limitations on Dividends

284. The last chapter in the Companies Act, Chapter 32, concerns companies that may not, according to their articles of association, distribute more than a limited dividend to their shareholders. The idea behind this regulation is that such private companies could be an alternative in areas where public money is involved – such as health care and housing. The limitation is shown by three letters added to the business name of the company: *svb* (an abbreviation for *Särskild vinstutdelnings begränsning* – that is, special limitation on dividends) if it is does not follow already from the name of the company that it has this special character (Chapter 32, section 17).

There are only a very few rules that are applicable only to svb-companies. Concerning these, see paragraphs 263 et seq.

Chapter 4. The *Societas Europea*

285. The *Societas Europea* (SE) exists also in Sweden according to what is stated in the Council Regulation (EC) Number. 2157/2001 on the Statute for a European Company. Sweden has issued the necessary additional legislation through a 2004 Act on the SE and a 2006 Act on worker influence in such companies.

From the regulation, it follows that an SE-company is a legal person with a share capital divided into shares. No shareholder is liable for the debts of the company – the maximum a shareholder can lose is what has been paid for the shares. The capital must be expressed in EUR, and its minimum is EUR 120,000. For additional rules concerning the share capital and the shares, the rules of the 2005 Companies Act are applicable.

An SE-company shall have its domicile in a state that is a member of the EU. Its domicile and main office must be situated in the same Member State. However, it is possible to move the domicile from one Member State to another. The business name of an SE-company must contain the abbreviation SE.

An SE-company can be formed in five different ways. Common to them all is that the SE-company is formed by already existing national artificial persons. Thus, natural persons cannot form an SE-company.

An SE-company is registered in a special register for such companies. The highest internal body is the shareholders' general meeting. As to the question of how the management shall be organized, it is up to the company itself to decide whether it shall use a monistic or a dualistic model.

The monistic model means that there is just one body that is responsible for the management and business of the company. The members of this body are elected by the general meeting. The national legislation may prescribe that there shall also be a managing director.

In the dualistic system, there are two bodies in addition to the general meeting – that is, one managing body and one supervisory body. In this system, it is the task of the supervisory body to elect and dismiss the members of the managing body, while it is the task of the general meeting to elect the members of the supervisory body and to control how the managing is done. However, it is possible to use managing directors also in this system.

The regulation contains rules on quorum and necessary majority for the different bodies.

As to auditing, the regulation does not contain any detailed rules.

The Swedish Act on SE-companies contains rules for the protection of the creditors when an SE-company moves from Sweden to another country. Further, the Act states that all SE-companies with their domiciles in Sweden shall have managing directors with responsibility for the day-to-day activities. In companies organized according to the dualistic system, the managing director shall be under the supervision of both the board and the supervisory body. The Act also contains rules on the minimum number of members of different kinds of boards. Thus, the board of directors/the managing body shall consist of at least three members and the supervisory body of at least five. Since the 2005, Swedish Companies Act does not contain any rules on a supervisory body, the Act on SE-companies states which rules in the Companies Act are to be used for supervisory bodies and their members. The Act on SE-companies also contains some extra rules on general meetings.

Part II. Partnerships

Chapter 1. Different Types of Partnership

§1. Different Forms in Swedish Law

286. As already indicated in the Introduction, there are three forms of partnership covered by the 1980 Partnerships Act: the simple – formerly, the non-trading – partnership (*enkla bolaget*), the trading partnership (*handelsbolaget*) and the limited partnership (*kommanditbolaget*). To these three is sometimes added the silent partnership (*tysta bolaget*).

§2. Basic Distinguishing Features

287. According to the Partnerships Act, the simple partnership is the basic form (Chapter 1, section 3). It comes into existence as soon as two or more natural or artificial persons have agreed to cooperate for a common purpose and the agreement includes a requirement that there be some kind of undertaking from each partner.

The agreement may be in writing, but an oral agreement satisfies the law and so, incidentally, does any behaviour by a person that shows that he/she has made an agreement (*konkludent* (conclusive) behaviour in Swedish).

It is not usually difficult to decide whether a common purpose exists, but if there is any doubt, it is ascertained by determining whether, according to the agreement, the outcome of the cooperation – usually a profit – is to be divided between those who cooperate. This is the most typical of all common purposes. But the common responsibility of those who cooperate for the losses also indicates a common goal. It is not necessary for the common purpose to be to benefit the partners financially; an altruistic purpose is also accepted as the goal of any kind of partnership.

Other circumstances that can be checked when investigating whether or not a common purpose exists include whether those who are cooperating have a right to be involved in managing the activities of the 'organization' or to control its activities; both these factors are, in Swedish law, circumstances that speak in favour of a common purpose. So, too, does the fact that the organization has an economic basis of its own (assets of some kind). If all these circumstances are not enough, finally, one can also take into account what the organization is called by those cooperating: *bolag* (i.e., partnership) or something else. This alone is not decisive, but it might reveal the intention of the cooperating parties.

As for the undertakings of those cooperating, they may, for example, put money, other property or their services into the use of the common interest. These contributions need not be of the same size or of the same kind. It is not unusual for one partner to contribute his/her personal services, while another contributes the necessary financial resources.

288. These three conditions – an agreement, a common purpose and an undertaking – are used for delimiting purposes. A loan could come close to a partnership, but the lender has the right to a fixed rate of interest and not a profit dependent on the outcome of the activities. Even if the lender has been promised a small bonus in the form of a share of the profits that might result from the activities of the borrower, the relationship between the parties is still looked upon as a loan and not as a partnership.

As for distinguishing a partnership from an employer–employee relationship, a share in the profits is an essential factor. The fact that an employed person receives a bonus payment that depends on the sales or the profit from the activities of the enterprise for which he/she works does not change the character of an employment relationship to a partnership. It is important to observe in this connection that Swedish labour law includes a large number of rules for the benefit of the weaker party, the employee, and the courts will not accept the transformation of an employer–employee relationship into a partnership unless they are convinced that the activities in question really are to be characterized as a partnership.

What has been said with respect to employment is equally true with regard to leases of land and rental agreements. Landowners and landlords might prefer to arrange a lease or a rental agreement as a partnership, but such attempts will fail unless – when the question is brought before a court – the court is convinced that a partnership really does exist. This, too, is an area of law where the weaker party has been afforded numerous protective measures that are not to be found in partnership law. But if one person contributes his/her land and another person his/her labour and the activities of these two persons result in something that is in fact common to them both – for example, profits to be divided equally between them – then partnership law should apply.

Another legal relationship that sometimes comes close to a partnership is joint ownership. There is in Sweden a separate Joint Ownership Act from 1904, designed to solve problems connected with the administration and dissolution of joint ownership of land, chattels, and so on. A distinguishing feature is often that a basic agreement is lacking in a joint ownership situation – one of the objectives of the 1904 Act is to offer solutions when, for example, the owners of something lack such an agreement. But sometimes a basic agreement exists without the parties to that agreement either having formed a partnership – with solutions to different problems available in the Partnerships Act – or having solved the problems that later arise. The line between a partnership and joint ownership is drawn with the help of the three prerequisites that must exist for there to be a partnership (see *supra*).

289. As pointed out in the Introduction, in Sweden companies and partnerships are dealt with in the law of associations together with cooperative societies and non-profit associations (non-profit member organizations). A common feature of all these organizations is that they are based on an agreement between a number of cooperating persons (with the exception, however, of the one-man company; see paragraph 21 *supra*) who have joined together for a purpose that is common to all those who are cooperating. A demand for some kind of undertaking might also be found in all of them. This means that sometimes a problem arises in distinguishing between partnerships, on the one hand, and cooperative societies and non-profit associations, on the other. Normally, this problem is solved by looking at the basic agreement. If according to this agreement – which is sometimes referred to as the articles of association, the by-laws, or the like – new participants can become members without any amendment of the agreement and if a member can leave the organization without such an amendment, then the organization is not a partnership, but either a cooperative society or a non-profit association. If, on the other hand, the basic agreement needs an amendment when a new member is accepted or an old member leaves, then the organization is to be characterized as a partnership. It should be added that this way of distinguishing partnerships from cooperative societies and non-profit associations does not always work, and there are other delimiting factors that can be used when this proves necessary.

An organization that is not normally difficult to distinguish from a partnership – although in Sweden it is often dealt with in the law of associations (which obviously is not quite correct from a formal point of view) – is the foundation (*stiftelse*). It does not have any members and thus cannot itself be a partnership.

§3. Distinguishing Different Types of Partnership

290. What have been defined so far is a simple partnership, which, incidentally, is not a legal person, but only a contractual relationship between the partners (the Partnerships Act, Chapter 1, section 4). It cannot do business in its own right, but since 1995, it can be used for different forms of trading.

291. What else is needed, then, to transform a partnership into a trading partnership?

A trading partnership is intended to engage in business activities. It can do business in its own right. It is, in other words, a legal person (Chapter 1, section 1). A partnership becomes a trading partnership when – in the words of the Partnerships Act (Chapter 1, section 1) – two or several persons have agreed to do business in common in a partnership and the partnership is registered as such.

'Business' means simply business in the normal sense of professional activities of an economic kind. A consortium between the shareholders of a company on how they will vote at the shareholders' meetings of that company (a voting agreement) is not a business activity, and such a consortium will therefore be characterized as a simple partnership (if it is not a non-profit association; see paragraph 290 *supra*).

As for the requirement that the business be done in common, this is a requirement that was of importance when a trading company came into effect just by doing business in common – which was the case before 1995. One example of such cooperation that was discussed at some length in the Swedish Parliament in connection with the adoption of the 1980 Partnerships Act was situation where a number of companies entered into a consortium agreement for a special project. However, the provision that a trading partnership does not come into effect unless it is registered as such in the trade register (which is kept by the Companies Registration Office) has made the requirement that its business be done in common superfluous. In other words, a trading partnership – just like a company limited by shares – does not come into being and become a legal person until it is registered.

292. Pension funds and staff funds created according to the provisions in the 1967 Act on safeguarding pension commitments may not (as of 1 July 2005) be partners in a trading partnership (Chapter 1, section 2a).

293. According to the Partnerships Act, Chapter 1, section 2, a limited partnership is a trading partnership where one or more partners – but not all of them – have entered into the partnership on the condition that they are not personally liable for the debts of the partnership. Such a partnership is founded in the same way as a normal trading partnership – two or more persons enter into an agreement to form a limited partnership and have it registered. Neither a foundation (*stiftelse*) nor a non-profit association (*ideell förening*) may enter into the agreement as a personally liable partner; if this happens, the partnership will be a normal trading partnership and not a limited partnership (Chapter 3, section 2).

294. The silent partnership is not dealt with in the 1980 Partnerships Act. One of the leading authorities on Swedish company and partnership law – Professor Håkan Nial – has advocated that Swedish law accept the existence of the silent partnership: that is, a kind of partnership that is characterized by one person (A) putting money into the business of another person (B) in such a way that the money is absorbed in B's business, but on the condition that A will share in any profit or loss and maybe also have some influence on the activities of the enterprise. B is thus the owner of what the silent partner has put into the activities, which is the typical feature of the silent partnership. This form of partnership is not expressly encountered in any Supreme Court or Court of Appeal reports, but there is a decision of the Supreme Administrative Court (*regeringsrätten*) in which that court seems to have accepted the possibility of the existence of a silent partnership.

However, there will be no further comment on silent partnerships in this account.

Chapter 2. Simple Partnerships

§1. Legal Personality

295. As already mentioned, a simple partnership is not a legal person, only a contractual relationship between the partners (Chapter 1, section 4).

296. A simple partnership is not registered in any trade register. However, the partners of some simple partnerships are themselves registered according to the rules of the 1974 Trade Registers Act (section 2).

297. Even if a simple partnership is not a legal person, it can nowadays be used for trading purposes. For such activities, economic resources are, of course, needed. These can be obtained at least to a certain degree by the use in the partners' activities of property belonging to the partners individually, but sometimes the property used in the partnership must be characterized as jointly owned. For such jointly owned property, the 1904 Joint Ownership Act is not applicable. The co-owners should not use this property or any part of it for their own benefit unless the other partners agree. On the contrary, it should be used to pay any debts that arise through the activities of the partnership. The question to what degree a partner can sell or pledge his/her share in the jointly owned property is one on which opinions differ in the Swedish legal literature. With regard to the position of an individual partner's creditors, on the other hand, there is a decision of the Supreme Court that shows that a partner's share in jointly owned property can be distrained. And if a partner is adjudged bankrupt, the bankrupt's estate includes the partner's gross value of common assets – the other partners have to lodge proof of their claims in the same way as other creditors.

This uncertainty with regard to the law in the area of jointly owned property makes the simple partnership a somewhat uncertain alternative, even though the Partnerships Act makes this form of partnership a possible alternative for different kinds of business activity.

§2. Questions of Liability

298. A simple partnership is – as have just been mentioned – not a legal person. Rights and obligations that arise during the activities of the partnership are therefore the rights and obligations of the individual partners and not of the partnership. The Partnerships Act states in Chapter 4, section 5, that an agreement (contract) that is concluded for the partners or under a designation referring to the partners jointly entails contractual rights and obligations only for the partner(s) who has (have) entered into the agreement.

299. But even if the main rule of the Partnerships Act is that only the contracting partner becomes liable, other rules imply that this main rule is not as stringent as one might first believe. First, a proxy by one partner makes another partner – the mandator – also liable. And proxies are common. A common form of proxy is a letter of authorization, which should be shown by the authorized person to the third party. But a proxy can also be given in writing or orally by the authorizing person to a third party. In these cases, the authority of the authorized person depends on the contents of the proxy: limiting internal instructions do not bind a third party who is acting in good faith. Another form of authorization is an oral proxy from the mandator to the authorized person; here the third party will not secure better rights in relation to the mandator than those that follow from the authorization. But the form of proxy that is probably the most common, and therefore the most important, in simple partnerships is that conferred on a person because of the position he/she holds. If someone holds a position that is accompanied, by law or custom, by a certain authority to act on behalf of another person, the former is empowered to act in law within the limits of this authority. If, for example, two farmers in a simple partnership employ a steward (land agent), the latter holds such a proxy as is common for a person in that position. If one of the two farmers becomes the steward, he/she holds the same kind of proxy and is thus empowered to bind both himself/herself and his/her partner.

It should be added that a proxy can also develop through conduct showing that someone accepts another person as his/her legal representative, through (in Swedish) *konkludent* (conclusive) conduct.

An agreement entered into with a third party through a representative holding a proxy must be made on behalf of the partner(s) if he/she/they is (are) to be bound. But if any partner is bound, he/she has the same rights in relation to the other party as a party who has entered into the agreement himself/herself, and he/she is jointly and severally responsible and liable.

300. This is not the only situation when a partner becomes personally liable even when he/she does not enter into an agreement personally. Joint and several liability is laid down by the Partnerships Act (Chapter 4, section 6) if a partner makes an agreement with a third party and in that agreement uses a designation by which the partners are jointly denominated and that includes any of the words *handelsbolag* (trading partnership), *aktiebolag* (company limited by shares), *förening* (society or association) or *stiftelse* (foundation), on the condition, however, that the other partner(s) know(s) that this designation was used and that the third party was not aware (neither knew nor should have understood) that the designation related to a simple partnership.

§3. Contributions and Division of Profits

301. A simple partnership does not exist unless the cooperating persons have undertaken to put something into the organization. But these items can be different, and they can also be of differing value. It all depends on what the partners have agreed.

302. Interest on the contributions that the partners have made will not be credited to the partners unless they have agreed otherwise. This is probably not very uncommon, for example, in farming partnerships. The same is true with regard to remuneration for administration by a partner. If interest and/or remuneration is to be credited to the different partners, however, it seems natural for annual accounts to be drawn up with the net result for the year to be calculated after interest and remuneration have been deducted.

303. How the net profit (or loss) is to be divided is sometimes stated in the partnership agreement. It is not necessary for the partners to have the same right to share in the profit; it is even possible for only some of the partners to share the profit, while other partners have no such right at all – the purpose of a partnership is not necessarily economic (it can be altruistic) or directly economic (the economic advantages can be indirect). If the agreement does not state how the profit is to be divided between the partners, it should be divided equally between them.

304. If annual accounts are drawn up – which is often the situation only with regard to simple partnerships engaged in business activities – the partners are to receive their interest, remuneration and profit annually if their agreement does not stipulate otherwise. A partner is not obliged to increase his/her contribution above what has been agreed upon in the partnership agreement. No partner can, during the existence of the partnership, demand payment directly from another partner for his/her costs in the partnership or for his/her administration fee or interest. But he/she can demand payment for these costs from the jointly owned property that might be found in the partnership (see paragraph 297 *supra*). If he/she is himself/herself in charge of such property, he/she can recover his/her costs from it. All these rules are subject to the partners not having agreed otherwise.

305. The partners are obliged to be loyal to each other.

§4. The Management of a Simple Partnership

306. The partners have the right to decide themselves how their partnership is to be managed. Not uncommonly, the circumstances show which partner is supposed to do what.

307. If nothing else is agreed upon, the Partnerships Act states (Chapter 4, section 3) that all partners must agree on decisions concerning internal management. However, if for some urgent reason a decision has to be made although all the partners cannot participate in it – one of the partners may be ill or have gone abroad – the Act allows such a decision to be made anyhow.

A partner who has not been deprived of his/her right to participate in the management of the partnership has a right to veto a decision that another partner intends to make. This right of veto, however, may not be used in such a way that it contravenes the partner's obligation to show loyalty towards his/her fellow partners. If according to the agreement between the partners one or some of them is (are) responsible for management, such an agreement will often be taken to mean that the other partners have no right to participate in the management and also no right to veto the decisions of those who are in charge of management.

308. Even a partner who does not take part in the management of the partnership's activities has the right to check the accounts of the partnership and to obtain the information concerning its activities that he/she requires. This right can, however, be withheld from any partner of a simple partnership through a clause in the partnership agreement. If such a clause proves to be unreasonable, however, it can be set aside by a court in response to an action by the partner in question.

309. With regard to accounts, the simple partnership is not required to maintain accounting records. But the partners are required to do so, according to the 1999 Accounting Act, if they are carrying on business. These rules are connected with tax legislation. So, too, are the obligations for all natural and artificial persons to keep such records as are necessary for them to fulfil their obligations in connection with their own tax returns. Apart from this and with regard to the internal relations within the partnership, the obligation of the partner(s) in charge of management to keep records depends on the individual kind of partnership – a partner in charge of a partnership has to see to it that he/she is able to provide his/her fellow partners with such information as is needed for them to gain an acceptable picture of the status of the partnership.

310. As for relations with third parties, each partner can in principle only bind himself/herself (see paragraphs 298 et seq. *supra*).

§5. Transferability of Participations

311. The acceptance of a new partner presupposes the approval of all the old partners unless the partners have agreed otherwise in the partnership agreement.

As for the situation when a partner wishes to leave a simple partnership, see paragraph 312 *infra*.

If a partner wishes to transfer or pledge the economic rights that have evolved from his/her partnership, such action is probably possible if the partnership agreement accepts it. But the partnership agreement can probably also include a right of redemption for the other partners in such a situation.

§6. Liquidation

312. With regard to grounds for winding-up simple partnerships, the Partnerships Act, Chapter 4, section 7, refers to the grounds for winding-up trading partnerships – see paragraph 357 et seq. *infra* – with one exception: The provisions on the winding-up of one-man trading partnerships do not apply to simple partnerships. (If one of two partners leaves, the partnership is assumed to have ceased to exist when the partner left.) This means that if the partners have not agreed on a fixed period for the existence of the partnership, any partner has the right to give notice of termination whenever he/she wishes; the partnership will then go into liquidation six months later if the partners have not agreed on a different – shorter or longer – period. But even if the partnership agreement is entered into for a fixed time, a partner has the right to bring the partnership into liquidation when another partner has essentially neglected his/her obligations under the partnership agreement or when there is any other important ground for winding-up the partnership. Normally, the death of a partner and a partner's becoming bankrupt are also grounds for the winding-up of a partnership. The Partnerships Act, however, contains provisions that might make it possible for a partnership to continue even where there is a reason for winding it up.

To this, however, it should be added that a simple partnership might have been entered into for a specific temporary purpose, but without any specific period for the existence of the partnership being given in the partnership agreement. If this is the case, the partnership will probably be deemed to have been formed for a fixed period.

313. Internal relations between the partners during the liquidation process can be arranged in whatever way the partners wish – as long as they agree or have agreed in the partnership agreement. The Partnerships Act contains rules to cover the situation where such agreements do not exist: Normally, all partners must agree on decisions concerning internal management; an exception is made for decisions that have to be made for urgent reasons; any partner has the right to check the accounts of the partnership in liquidation and to obtain information concerning its activities. As for relations with third parties, each partner represents himself/herself. But if they act together, they will be jointly and severally liable.

314. The liquidation process is normally very simple. Jointly owned property, however, sometimes has to be sold.

If it is probable that liquidation is being unreasonably delayed or is otherwise harming the interests of a partner, the appropriate court may appoint one or several liquidators to carry out the liquidation.

When the partners are responsible for liquidation of the partnership, the liquidation process ends with an agreement in writing. If the court has appointed one or more liquidators, the latter submit a liquidation instrument when their job is completed.

§7. Taxation

315. The partners of a simple partnership are treated in the same way as other individual taxpayers – natural persons as natural persons and artificial persons as artificial persons. The income tax on trade for a natural person is approximately 31% on incomes up to approximately SEK 430,200, approximately 51% for incomes over that figure and up to approximately SEK 616,100 and approximately 56% for incomes over that figure. To this tax, however, must be added both different kinds of social security contributions and other payroll taxes; thus, the total tax on a natural person who is a partner in a simple partnership engaged in trade is usually (exemptions are, for example, granted for older persons) higher than 31%, 51% and 56%. As for companies that are partners, see paragraph 272 *supra*, where taxation of companies is considered.

It should finally be added that what is said here on taxation is based on the situation in December 2014 and that taxation is an area where legislation is very often amended.

Chapter 3. Trading Partnerships

§1. Legal Personality

316. Until the end of 1994, a trading partnership was a legal person as soon as it was founded – that is, from the moment when the partners agreed to form it. As of 1995, a trading partnership, however, comes into existence only upon registration (the Partnerships Act, Chapter 1, section 1).

The fact that a trading partnership is a legal person means that it acquires rights and assumes obligations itself and also that it can be a party to legal actions before courts and other authorities.

317. Under the 1974 Trade Registers Act, the application for registration must be signed by all the partners. The authority responsible for keeping trade registers is Companies Registration Office.

The details that have to be submitted for registration include the corporate identity number and the business name of the partnership, the nature of its business activities, the county and the place where its main office is located as well as its postal address, the full names of all the partners as well as their identity numbers and addresses, who is to sign for the partnership and in what manner if each partner is not to sign individually (which will be the rule where nothing is said to the contrary in the trade register) and also the name, identity number (or, if such number is lacking, date of birth) and address of the auditor when the partnership is – according to law – obliged to have a qualified accountant.

The business name of a partnership must include the word *handelsbolag*. If the partnership has a secondary business name, this name may not include either *handelsbolag* or *kommanditbolag* (limited partnership). The name must be clearly distinguishable from other business names previously entered and still registered.

Any change regarding the information that has been registered must immediately be filed for registration by all the partners. If a partner has died, the other partners have a duty to file the amendment. When a liquidator has been appointed by the court, he/she becomes responsible for filing for registration. Any partner who has left the partnership has, in addition to the registration that must be undertaken by the remaining partners, the right to register that he/she is no longer a partner (the Trade Registers Act, section 13, paragraph 3).

Failing to register with and providing incorrect information to the registration authority are offences and accordingly punishable.

§2. Questions of Liability

318. The trading partnership is, as the legal person it is, liable for its own debts. But liability is not confined to the partnership as such – all the partners are jointly and severally liable for the debts of the partnership (Partnerships Act, Chapter 2, section 20). Any creditor can choose to demand payment for any debt of the partnership from whomever he/she wishes – the partnership or any or all of the partners. This has been deemed to be of value not only to creditors, but also to partnerships and their partners, since it makes it easier for partnerships to obtain credit.

The fact that the partners have the same liability as the partnership means that the partners often have the same responsibility as the partnership with regard to other obligations as well. But an obligation to perform something can sometimes only be met by the partnership, and then the partners are liable only in damages. And in certain situations, other circumstances may make it clear that the partners are not under the same obligation as the partnership.

Since the responsibility and liability of the partners are the same as that of the partnership, the partners can normally rely on limitations in the responsibility and liability of the partnership. If, for example, a third party has released the partnership from its liability, then this third party normally cannot demand payment from the partners.

With regard to the possibility of offsetting one amount against another, different situations may arise. If a creditor of the partnership demands payment from a partner, this partner can use any counterclaim belonging to the partnership against the creditor. He/she can also use his/her own counterclaim against the creditor's claim, but not that of another partner. If a creditor demands payment from the partnership, the partnership can use its own counterclaim, but not that of a partner unless the partner agrees. If the partnership demands payment from a debtor, the debtor cannot use his/her counterclaim against a partner as payment. If a partner's creditor demands payment from him/her, he/she cannot use a claim that the partnership has against the creditor as a counterclaim. If a partner demands payment for his/her personal claim from a third party, this debtor can use a claim that he/she has against the partnership as a counterclaim.

If a court has delivered a judgment according to which the partnership is not liable, this will also free the partners. If, on the other hand, the partnership has been declared liable in a judgment, that judgment cannot as such be used for execution against a partner, but it will no doubt have an indirect influence on any later judgment against the partner.

319. As for the situation where a new partner joins the partnership, the Partnerships Act states in Chapter 2, section 22, that the new partner is also liable for the debts that existed when he/she joined the partnership. When a partner leaves the partnership, the Act prescribes, on the other hand, that he/she is liable for the debts that existed when he/she left, but not for any debts that arise thereafter, providing that the third party knew or should have known that he/she had left (Chapter 2, section 22).

320. A partnership can go into bankruptcy on its own petition or on the petition of its creditors. It is evident that the creditors of the individual partners cannot make any claims on the bankruptcy estate of the partnership. But should the creditors of the bankruptcy estate of the partnership be allowed to make their claims against the bankruptcy estate(s) of the individual partner(s)? This question is answered by the Partnerships Act, Chapter 2, section 20. This section states that the creditors of the partnership shall not get more from the bankruptcy estate(s) of the individual partner(s) than the sum they are unable to obtain from the bankruptcy estate of the partnership. The same approach applies if the partnership has not gone into bankruptcy, but the partners have.

321. A partner may have a claim against the partnership, for example, for something that he/she has sold to it. If he/she is paid before the partnership is declared bankrupt, he/she will keep his/her payment unless it is later recovered to the bankruptcy estate. As for competition for payment from the bankruptcy estate between a partner and other creditors, the law is probably that no partner may compete with the creditors of the partnership in its bankruptcy estate. He/she will receive payment only if there is a surplus after these creditors have been paid.

§3. Contributions and Division of Profits

322. When the partnership agreement is entered into, the partners might transfer money and other property to it as their agreed contributions. The partnership often becomes the owner, but it is also possible that a partner's contribution is a lease of property.

The partnership may incidentally also buy or rent necessary items from the partners without there being any connection with their contributions.

Whether an object that a partner has transferred to the partnership is to be regarded as a contribution or not depends on what the partners have agreed. What the partners have agreed to contribute in the basic agreement will normally be looked upon as their contributions.

323. The agreed amounts to be contributed cannot usually be changed unless all the partners agree. Thus, one partner can neither increase nor decrease his/her agreed contribution unless the other partners agree. If the partnership agreement states that a majority of the partners have the right to amend the partnership agreement, however, this is in principle valid.

If a partner does not make his/her contribution on time, he/she is obliged under the Partnerships Act, Chapter 2, section 13, to pay interest from the day that the contribution should have been made.

324. As have already been mentioned, partnerships may be founded for altruistic goals or for the purpose of improving the partners' economic interests in other ways than through a division of profits. Normally, however, the goal of a partnership is to achieve a profit to be distributed among the partners. The partners are free to decide according to what principles this distribution is to be carried out. If nothing else is agreed upon, any profit is to be divided in equal shares between the partners (Partnerships Act, Chapter 2, section 8). It is not unusual, though, for the partnership agreement to state that the profit is to be distributed according to the size of the contributions made by the different partners. Whatever has been decided for the yearly division of profits will also – if nothing else is agreed upon – determine the distribution of the final profit at the time of liquidation of the partnership.

The Partnerships Act states that each partner has a right to receive his/her share of the profit for each financial year as soon as the accounts for the year have been prepared (Chapter 2, section 9).

325. If the accounts for one financial year show a loss, this loss is to be divided between the partners according to the same principles as would have governed the division of a profit unless the partners have agreed otherwise (Partnerships Act, Chapter 2, section 8).

326. If there has been a loss, the capital contributed by the individual partners might be less than their agreed contributions, and the difference will then be made up out of the interest and the fee that the partner would otherwise have received for the financial year in question unless the partners have agreed or agree differently (Partnerships Act, Chapter l, section 9).

§4. The Management of a Trading Partnership

327. Concerning management, the Partnerships Act deals separately with the internal management of a partnership and the right to represent the partnership in relation to third parties.

I. Internal Management

328. With regard to internal management, the Act states (Chapter 2, section 1) that the partners may in their partnership make an agreement or otherwise decide whatever they wish with one exception: Any partner has the right to inspect the accounts of the partnership and to receive information about its business (on the condition, however, that this right of scrutiny is not exercised at such a time or in such a way that it seriously inconveniences the partnership). See Partnerships Act, Chapter 2, section 5. This right of inspection has been deemed necessary in an organization where the partners are personally and severally liable for the debts.

It can be added that the details of a partnership agreement can, under ordinary contract law, be adjusted or the agreement itself be set aside if a court finds that such details cause unreasonable hardship for a party to it (*oskäligt avtalsvillkor*).

329. According to the Partnerships Act, Chapter 2, section 3 (and unless the partners have agreed otherwise), every partner has the right to take any action in the internal management of the partnership unless such action is vetoed by another partner who is not, under the partnership agreement, deprived of the right to take part in the management of the partnership. The rule that each partner has the right to take such action as he/she deems necessary is based on the presumption that it is a normal rule in partnerships and also that it makes quick decision making possible. But the duty to show loyalty towards the other partners should make a partner inform his/her co-partners about important decisions concerning internal management.

The right to participate in management is a personal right of the individual partner: It cannot be transferred to some other person, and a partner may not use an agent unless the partners have agreed otherwise. But it seems natural for a partner who is involved in the management of the partnership to be allowed to use one or more assistants if this is necessary for him/her to carry out his/her work.

330. As mentioned in the preceding paragraph, those partners who are involved in the management of the partnership have a right of veto. The right to take part in management, however, can be taken away from a partner in an agreement between the partners. It is even possible for the partners to agree to abolish the right of veto for partners who are not deprived of their right to take part in the management of a partnership.

331. A veto is not the only limitation that might exist concerning the right of a partner to make internal decisions. Other limitations follow from the prohibition on the individual partners to act contrary to the kind of activity for which the partnership was formed or contrary to the purpose it is to fulfil (see Partnerships Act, Chapter 2, section 3).

The partners have agreed on what kind of activity their partnership is to engage in – see *supra* paragraph 317 concerning registration in the trade register – and this agreement binds them all. This is not to say that any activity outside a very strict reading of the agreement is against the law, but acts that are not related to the agreed area of activity have to be agreed upon by all the partners. A partnership may nevertheless invest its capital in suitable bonds and take similar action.

The purpose of the partnership is also binding, however. If, as is normally the case, the purpose of the partnership's business is to make profits for the partners, then other purposes are against the law – with one exception: A partner who has the right to act on behalf of the partnership may make gifts for purposes of public benefit or of a similar nature, provided that such gifts are of minor importance with regard to the financial position of the partnership (Partnerships Act, Chapter 2, section 3).

Another rule that the partners have to observe is the rule of equal treatment, which means that all the partners have the same rights and obligations unless the Partnerships Act or the partnership agreement states otherwise. Legal transactions and other measures that are likely to give undue advantage to a partner or a third party to the detriment of the partnership or other partners are probably also forbidden (the general clause of Swedish association law).

332. The partners can agree on other forms of management than that described above, provided that they all agree. It is even possible to form a board of directors. But the Partnerships Act does not regulate such a structure, and it might cause serious problems later if the board makes decisions that other partners find more or less unacceptable. There are no mandatory provisions in the Partnerships Act corresponding to the rules protecting individual shareholders and minorities that the Companies Act contains, but one, namely the right to scrutinize the account of the partnership and receive information about its business (the Partnerships Act, Chapter 2, section 5).

333. It should be added that the Partnerships Act, Chapter 2, section 3, deals with the situation where two or more partners are jointly responsible for management and a decision has to be made for some urgent reason, even though the prescribed number of partners cannot participate. Where a decision cannot be delayed without considerable inconvenience to the partnership and a partner is prevented from attending by sickness or some similar reason, the other partner(s) may, unless the partners have agreed otherwise, make the necessary decision.

334. If the partnership agreement prescribes that a partner is responsible for the management or part of the management of the partnership, this partner may neither be removed from his/her position nor leave it without an important reason unless the partners have agreed otherwise (Partnerships Act, Chapter 2, section 4).

335. For each financial year, each partner is to be credited with both interest on his/hers investment in the partnership and a reasonable fee for his/her management of the activities of the partnership (Partnerships Act, Chapter 2, section 6). The partners may, however, agree otherwise regarding this matter, too.

336. Rules concerning the accounts and annual reports of trading partnerships are to be found in the 1999 Accounting Act and the 1995 Annual Reports Act. The Accounting Act states that all trading partnerships are required to maintain accounting records and also that all trading partnerships have to produce either annual accounts or annual reports. Annual accounts consist of an income statement and a balance sheet. Small partnerships (i.e., partnerships with a net turnover not exceeding SEK 3 million) may produce their annual accounts in a simplified form. Annual reports consist, on the other hand, of an income statement, a balance sheet, notes and an administration report. In larger partnerships, the annual report shall also include a cash flow analysis. The annual accounts do not become public, but the annual reports do.

The trading partnerships that are obliged to produce annual reports in three different situations (the Accounting Act of 1999, Chapter 6, section 1):

(1) If one or more legal persons are partners in the trading partnership.
(2) If the trading partnership satisfy more than one of the following conditions:
    (a) the median number of employees of the partnership during each of the two most recent financial years has exceeded fifty;
    (b) the reported balance sheet total of the partnership for each of the two most recent financial years has exceeded SEK 40 million; and
    (c) the reported net turnover of the partnership for each of the two most recent financial years has exceeded SEK 80 million.
(3) The trading partnership is the parent of o group that satisfy more than one of the following conditions:
    (a) the median number of employees of the partnership during each of the two most recent financial years has exceeded fifty;
    (b) the reported balance sheet total of the partnership for each of the two most recent financial years has exceeded SEK 40 million; and

(c) the reported net turnover of the partnership for each of the two most recent financial years has exceeded SEK 80 million.

Whether the trading partnership is a parent of a group or not, follows by the definition in the Annual Reports Act of 1995 (Chapter 1, section 4)

Both the annual accounts and the annual report have to be signed by all the partners. If one of the partners has a dissenting opinion, that opinion may be attached.

The Accounting Act and the Annual Reports Act state, among other things, the maximum value at which current and fixed assets may be stated in the balance sheet, thus preventing trading partnerships from showing unrealistic profits. But the assets could also be stated below the allowed maximum, which in turn can cause problems for a partner if he/she does not get the share in the profit that he/she should get. This kind of problem can be avoided by stipulations regarding valuation principles in the partnership agreement. However, a court would probably be prepared to adjust a valuation if it resulted in unreasonable hardship for a partner.

The accounts should show both the contribution agreed to by each partner (in the partnership agreement) and his/her share in the partnership.

The day-to-day records for each financial year are to be summarized in the annual accounts, which must be recorded as soon as possible and not later than six months after the end of the financial year. The need to submit tax returns, however, may force the partners to have the annual accounts prepared sooner than six months after the end of the financial year. The partners are entitled to interest on their investment in the partnership, to management fees and to their shares in the profit for the year as soon as the annual accounts have been prepared (the Partnerships Act, Chapter 2, section 14). If the partners – or some of them – have been allowed to make withdrawals on account, these withdrawals are usually settled at this stage.

337. If a partner is of the opinion that the annual accounts are not correct, he/she may bring a legal action within one year of the date when the accounts were made available to him/her (Partnerships Act, Chapter 2, section 16). This action probably has to be brought against the partnership as such where the assets are recorded at too low a value or possibly not recorded at all, with the result that the profit for the year is too low. If the plaintiff's claim concerns only another or certain other partners, it might be sufficient for the action to be brought against these partners. There is nevertheless some uncertainty about this – it might be advisable to bring an action both against the partnership and against a partner who has received or been credited with too large an amount.

338. The fact that an action has been brought on the basis of the annual accounts does not always prevent the partners from receiving their interest, management fees and profits. The partners in charge of the funds of the partnership can pay out such sums as are not affected by the action. But they can also pay out other amounts if they are of the opinion that the action is unfounded. If they could not, one partner could in fact prevent his/her fellow partners from receiving any sums from the partnership for as long as his/her action takes – perhaps several years. The partner(s) making the decision to pay his/her/their fellow partners their interest, management fees and profits will be liable in damages only if the co-partners refuse to pay back what the court has ordered and his/her/their initial decision was taken wilfully or as a result of negligence.

339. As for monitoring of the partnership, the Partnerships Act does not contain any rules on auditing – the Act assumes that the partners will carry out the necessary checks themselves (see paragraph 328 *supra*). This right of scrutiny belongs to the partner personally, not to an agent that he/she might authorize, but if a person under age is a partner, he/she is represented by his/her legal representative, and so is any legal person that is a partner.

Although the Partnerships Act does not contain any rules on auditing, the 1999 Auditing Act does. This Act states that partnerships that are obliged to produce annual reports (see paragraph 336 *supra*) must also be audited by qualified auditors with certain exceptions for small-sized partnerships.

340. The Partnerships Act does not contain any provisions on disqualification because of possible bias. But it is nevertheless clear that a partner is not allowed to put his/her own interests before those of the partnership when the two conflict. This follows both from the requirement that the members of a partnership must be loyal towards each other and from the general clause presented above: No partner may enter into legal transactions or undertake other measures that are likely to give undue advantage to a partner or third party to the detriment of the partnership or other partners.

341. A problem closely connected with the question of disqualification is whether – and if so, to what degree – a partner may engage in business activities outside the partnership if these activities are in the same sector as those of the partnership. The Partnerships Act does not deal directly with this problem, but it follows from the ordinary obligations of a partner towards his/her partnership that there are limits on the degree to which he/she may engage in activities in the same area of business if these activities might cause damage to his/her partnership. The partner's position in the partnership, the management fee that he/she receives from the partnership and the like are related to his/her need for economic freedom of action.

342. A partner who wilfully or as a result of negligence causes the partnership to suffer damage when performing his/her duties will be liable for the damage to the partnership (see Partnerships Act, Chapter 2, section 14). Adequate causality is necessary, however – only damage that is a natural consequence of an act or omission will give rise to liability. The amount of damages may be reduced to a reasonable extent having regard to the nature of the action, the extent of the damage caused and other circumstances.

Two or more persons liable for the same damage are jointly and severally liable insofar as the liability of any of them has not been reduced in keeping with the conditions stated in the preceding passage. A person who has paid damages is entitled to reasonable reimbursement from the others, having regard to the circumstances.

343. The Partnerships Act does not contain any rules on a partner's liability towards a fellow partner or a third party who suffers damage.

344. An action (against one or more partners) for damages in favour of the partnership arising from a decision made or a measure undertaken during a given financial year must be initiated not later than one year after the annual report or the annual accounts are available to all the partners if the action is initiated in the name of the partnership (Partnerships Act, Chapter 2, section 15). If, however, the action is initiated in the name of one of the partners – that is, an *actio pro socio* – the time limit is one year after the annual report or the annual accounts become available to him/her. This alternative is open to partners who have neither management nor representation rights.

If the time for initiating an action has lapsed, such an action may nonetheless be initiated if the annual report or annual accounts or other information provided to the partners does not provide essentially correct and complete information concerning the decision or the measure that forms the basis for the action. Such an action may not, however, be initiated after the lapse of three years from the end of the financial year when the decision or measure concerned was made or undertaken.

An action for damages based on criminal liability may nevertheless be initiated within the normal period of limitation (i.e., usually ten years).

II. The Right to Represent the Partnership in Relation to Third Parties

345. The right to take action in the internal management of a partnership and the right to represent it vis-à-vis third parties may, but need not, agree.

The main rule of the Partnerships Act (Chapter 2, section 17) is that every partner is authorized to represent the partnership unless the partners have agreed otherwise (or the partnership is in liquidation; see concerning this situation paragraph 363 *infra*). According to this rule, even a partner who does not take part in internal management could represent the partnership, and a third party who has in good faith relied on the information in the registration file is protected. But usually such a partner will have no right of representation – the partners will have agreed on an exception and filed it in the trade register.

Apart from situations where the partners have agreed on an exception to the partners' right of representation, only a court can deprive a partner of his/her right of representation and then only if he/she has shown disloyalty in relation to the partnership (Partnerships Act, Chapter 2, section 17).

The partnership agreement can provide for whatever form of representation the partners consider best. The agreement can state that some of the partners – like a board of directors – shall have the right to authorize representatives – like *firmatecknare* (see paragraph 203 *supra*), that only some of the partners are to be authorized as representatives or, alternatively, that the partnership must be represented by two or several representatives together – *kollektiv firmateckningsrätt* (collective right of representation) in Swedish.

346. A partnership's entry in the trade register contains information on who is authorized to represent and bind it: The file either states what the agreement between the partners stipulates, or notes the decision of the court to deprive a partner of his/her right of representation, or says nothing at all about the right of representation. In the last case, the main rule applies: Every partner who is registered in the trade register is authorized to represent the partnership.

347. The right of representation concerns the partnership's relationship towards third parties. A representative cannot in that capacity change the partnership agreement or agree with individual partners as to their obligation to make contributions to the partnership. Nor can a representative enter into agreements with third parties concerning the internal relations of the partnership.

348. The Partnerships Act does not say anything about contracts between the partnership and the representative himself/herself. Whether or not the partnership will be bound in such situations depends on whether the contract is in accordance with or contrary to the purpose of the partnership, the activities that the partnership is to engage in, the principle of equal treatment and the general clause (see paragraph 331 *supra*).

349. But what happens when a representative of a partnership exceeds his/her competence? The answer to this question is that where a partner has exceeded his/her competence when entering into a legal transaction on behalf of the partnership, the partnership is not bound by the transaction if the other party realized or should have realized that this was the case (Partnerships Act, Chapter 2, section 18). In other words, a legal transaction entered into by a partner is normally valid because of the good faith of the third party. If, for example, a partner lacks the right to act in the internal management of the business of the partnership, but is still authorized to represent the partnership, he/she needs instructions from one of the partners who has the right to act in the internal management in order to represent the partnership. But he/she can bind the partnership even if he/she lacks such instructions and the third party was acting in good faith. Other examples include when a partner acts contrary to the purpose of the partnership or the activities that the partnership is to engage in and when a partner acts contrary to the principle of equal treatment or the general clause (see also the preceding paragraph).

350. The Partnerships Act states, in Chapter 2, section 19, that the partners can issue a signing authority of a special kind, a *prokura*, regulated in the 1974 Act on *prokura* (*prokuralag* 1974:158). If someone holds a proxy that is expressly called a *prokura* or if he/she is otherwise denominated a *prokurist* for somebody (i.e., the trade agent for – here – a partnership), then this trade agent may with very few exceptions represent and bind the partnership in relation to third parties. A *prokura* can be issued for two or more persons to be used by them jointly (*kollektivprokura*).

The issuance of a *prokura* is to be effected by all the partners unless they have agreed otherwise, while a *prokura* can be cancelled by each individual partner who has the right to represent the partnership in relation to third parties unless the partners have agreed otherwise.

A *prokura* need not be registered in the trade register.

If the *prokura* is a *kollektivprokura* and this restriction is registered, the restriction that it must be used jointly becomes public in relation to third parties. The cancellation of a registered *prokura* must also be registered.

The authority that a *prokurist* (trade agent) has under the 1974 Act cannot otherwise be restricted in relation to a third party who is acting in good faith.

351. Finally, it should be mentioned that a partnership can also be represented by agents in the same way as any natural or artificial person. The agent must be authorized – given his/her proxy – by a person with the right to represent the partnership. But here – as in other business activities – a common and important form of authorization is the proxy conferred on a person because of the position that he/she holds. If somebody holds a position from which there follows, by law or by custom, a certain authority to act on behalf of another (natural or artificial) person, the former is empowered to act in law within the limits of this authority (*ställningsfullmakt* in Swedish). A proxy can also develop through conduct that shows that someone accepts another person as his/her legal representative – through *konkludent* (conclusive) behaviour (i.e., through an implied authority).

§5. Transferability of Participations

352. A partner cannot transfer his/her membership in a partnership to a third party unless all the other partners agree, according to Chapter 2, section 2, of the Partnerships Act. This rule has been deemed to be the natural consequence of an organization in which all the partners are personally and severally liable for the debts. The partners have to know with whom they are cooperating.

This main rule is not mandatory, however. The partners may, if they wish, decide differently in the partnership agreement.

353. When, with the necessary permission of the other partner(s), one partner leaves and a new partner joins the partnership, the latter will normally assume the rights of the former. The change in the partnership must be registered in the trade register.

354. The partnership agreement may include the rule that the titleholders or some of the titleholders of a deceased partner shall or may become partners in lieu of the deceased partner. If such a clause is not included and the titleholder(s) of the deceased partner do not leave the partnership must go into liquidation. During the liquidation process, the estate of the deceased partner enters the partnership in liquidation.

The bankruptcy estate of a partner can also enter the partnership in liquidation.

355. But even if the transfer of the partnership as such usually presupposes that all the other partners agree, the Partnerships Act (Chapter 2, section 21) accepts the transfer of the economic rights of a partner to a third party without the consent of the other partner(s). The holder of these rights is entitled to receive what the partner would otherwise receive: interest on his/her contribution, management fee and the profit that he/she would have received according to the accounts. When the partnership is being liquidated, the holder of the economic right will receive the share that the partner would otherwise have received. The holder of the economic rights of a partner has the same right as the partner to give notice of termination.

The partner retains his/her obligations towards the partnership and the other partners even if he/she has transferred his/her economic rights.

356. The transfer of the economic rights from one partner to a third party might be seen as a problem for the remaining partners, who will be left with a partner who may not be as interested in the activities of the partnership as he/she would otherwise have been. To prevent such problems, the Partnerships Act (Chapter 2, section 21) provides that the partnership agreement may stipulate that partners or others shall have a right of pre-emption where the economic rights of a partner pass to a third party. Such a clause must state (1) the persons entitled to the right of pre-emption and whether certain kinds of acquisitions are to be exempted therefrom; (2) the order in which the right of pre-emption accrues to the persons entitled; (3) the period, not exceeding two months from the date when notice of the acquisition was given to the person entitled to the right of pre-emption, within which the person who wishes to exercise his/her right must notify the partnership thereof; and (4) the period, not exceeding one month from the date of the determination of the pre-emption price, within which the amount thereof shall be paid.

If the application of a provision of the partnership agreement concerning the determination of the pre-emption price would give undue advantage to any person, the price may be modified.

Except as otherwise provided in the partnership agreement, any dispute concerning the right of pre-emption and the determination of the pre-emption price in connection therewith is to be submitted to arbitration by three arbitrators under the 1999 Arbitration Act.

§6. Liquidation

I. Grounds for Winding-Up

357. The partners may, whenever they wish, unanimously decide that the partnership is to be wound up.

358. The partnership agreement may include a provision that sets out the period for which the partnership is to continue or that states the conditions under which it is to be wound up.

359. If the partnership agreement is concluded for a certain time, it cannot be wound up before the end of that time unless there is an important reason for doing so. The same is the case when the partnership agreement is concluded for a partner's life.

If the partnership agreement is concluded for an indefinite period, each partner has the right to give six months' notice unless the agreement states how long in advance notice must be given. The partnership is wound up when this six-month – or the agreed – period has expired. See the Partnerships Act, Chapter 2, section 24.

Notice must be given to all the partners.

360. The Partnerships Act also contains certain grounds for the winding-up of a partnership. The Act states that any partner has the right to demand that the partnership immediately go into liquidation if some other partner has materially neglected his/her obligations under the partnership agreement or if there is some other important ground for winding-up the partnership. This means that an important breach of the contract on the part of another partner is a ground for winding-up the partnership, but also that other important reasons, such as sickness on the part of any partner, may be sufficient reason for winding it up. The same applies if the kind of activity for which the partnership was formed becomes impossible. This clause in the Partnerships Act – Chapter 2, section 25 – is mandatory.

361. The Partnerships Act contains additional grounds for the winding-up of a partnership: the death of a partner (Chapter 2, section 26), the bankruptcy of a partner (Chapter 2, section 27) and the reduction of the number of partners to one (Chapter 2, section 28). In case of the death or bankruptcy of a partner, the partnership goes immediately into liquidation. When the number of partners has been reduced to one, the partnership automatically goes into liquidation six months later if the number of partners has not in the meantime increased to two or more.

362. The Partnerships Act contains provisions that might make it possible for a partnership to continue even when there is a reason for winding it up (except in the case of one-man partnerships). This might be effected through either the withdrawal or the expulsion of the partner to whom the ground for liquidation relates (Chapter 2, sections 29 and 30).

II. The Liquidation Process

363. The Partnerships Act (Chapter 2, section 31) states that actions in the internal management of a trading partnership in liquidation are to be taken by all the partners jointly unless they have agreed otherwise or one or more liquidators have been appointed by the court. Representation of the partnership in relation to third parties must also be undertaken jointly unless the partners have agreed otherwise or one or more liquidators have been appointed.

For the rest, the rules concerning management described above are to apply, with certain exceptions stated in the Act that are connected with the fact that subsequent activities are to have the aim of winding-up the partnership.

364. As already indicated, liquidation is sometimes taken care of by specially appointed liquidators. The Act thus prescribes that the appropriate court is to appoint one or more liquidators if it is probable that liquidation is being unreasonably delayed or otherwise conducted in such a way that the rights of one or more partners might be put in jeopardy (Partnerships Act, Chapter 2, section 37). When two or more liquidators are appointed, they are to act together unless the court states that – and how – the various tasks are to be divided between them (Partnerships Act, Chapter 2, section 38).

365. When the partners themselves are in charge of the liquidation process, they are to arrange for the distribution of the partnership's net assets in a document signed by all of them (Partnerships Act, Chapter 2, section 36).

When liquidators have been appointed and they have finished their work, they must, as soon as possible, submit a final account of their administration in the form of a liquidators' report covering the entire winding-up period. This final report must also contain particulars of the distribution of assets. Accounts for the entire winding-up period are to be attached to the report. The report and the accounts must be served upon each of the partners (Partnerships Act, Chapter 2, section 41).

366. When liquidators have been in charge of the winding-up of a partnership and one partner wishes to challenge the distribution, he/she must bring an action against the other partners within three months of being served with the liquidators' report (Partnerships Act, Chapter 2, section 43).

367. The partnership is dissolved when the partnership's net assets have been distributed or, if liquidators have been in charge of the winding-up, when the liquidators' report has been served on each of the partners (Partnerships Act, Chapter 2, section 44).

368. If, after the dissolution of the partnership, it appears that the partnership has further assets, or if an action is brought against the partnership, or if for any other reason a winding-up measure is needed, winding-up shall be resumed (Partnerships Act, Chapter 2, section 45).

§7. Taxation

369. Although the trading partnership is a legal person, it is the partners who are assessed for tax on its profits. No profit will result, however, unless the partners have received their agreed interest on the capital contributed and contractual management fees have been paid. Allowances for depreciation and reservations are also to be made before any division for tax purposes between the partners can take place. The division of the net income of the partnership between the partners then follows the same rules as govern the division of the profit of the partnership as such. Such a division can, however, be modified by the tax authority if it would cause an undue transfer of incomes from one partner to another. Such a situation could, in particular, arise in the case of spouses and of parents and children. In addition, there are certain rules concerning close partnerships aimed at preventing undue results – for example, where a partner has let his/her premises to the partnership at too high a rent.

Almost all income from a partnership is taxed as income from trade. This means that a natural person as partner pays approximately 31% tax on his/her income from the partnership up to an income of approximately SEK 420,800 (income from other sources included) and approximately 51% over that figure to approximately SEK 602,600, at which point the tax will be approximately 56%. In addition to these percentages, however, there are various kinds of social security contributions and other payroll taxes; these are deductible and amount, after deduction, to a minimum of approximately 10%. A company that is a partner, however, pays only 22% income tax.

When the ownership of a partnership passes to a new owner, it is necessary to decide whether it is the shares or the assets and liabilities of the partnership that are being transferred. A transfer of the shares could be favourable to the seller if he/she is a natural person (he/she will then often pay only 30% capital tax) and unfavourable to the buyer, while a transfer of the assets and liabilities might be favourable to the buyer.

It should finally be added that what is said in this paragraph on taxation is based on the situation in December 2014 and that taxation is an area where legislation is very often amended.

Chapter 4. Limited Partnerships

§1. Legal Personality

370. Under the Partnerships Act a limited partnership is a trading partnership that one or more partners – but not all of them – have entered into on the condition that he/she/they shall not be personally liable for the debts of the partnership (Chapter 1, section 3). A limited partnership does not come into effect until it is registered (see paragraphs 291 and 293 *supra*).

A partner with unlimited liability is in Swedish law called a *komplementär* (i.e., a general partner) and a partner with limited liability a *kommanditdelägare* (i.e., a limited partner).

371. With regard to registration of the limited partnership and amendments of the information registered, the same applies as for trading partnerships (see paragraph 317 *supra*). Some points need to be added, however. The business name of a limited partnership must include the word *kommanditbolag* (i.e., limited partnership in Swedish). A limited partner may not represent the limited partnership in relation to third parties, and, accordingly, he/she cannot be entered in the trade register as one of the persons who can sign on behalf of a *kommanditbolag*. The details filed in the trade register must include which partner(s) is (are) limited partner(s) and the amount that each such partner has undertaken to contribute to the partnership.

§2. Questions of Liability

372. The basic difference between a trading partnership and a limited partnership is that in a limited partnership not all the partners are personally liable. With regard to the personally liable partner or partners – that is, the general partner(s) – the points made earlier about partners in trading partnerships are applicable (Partnerships Act, Chapter 3, section 1), while the situation is different for the limited partners. The limited partner can only fulfil his/her obligation by making his/her contribution to the partnership, not by paying a creditor of the partnership (Partnerships Act, Chapter 3, section 8).

373. As already mentioned, neither a foundation (*stiftelse*) nor a non-profit association (*ideell förening*) may be a general partner. If they purport to be such a partner, the partnership will change its character and become a trading partnership; all of whose partners are liable in the way described above (Partnerships Act, Chapter 3, section 2).

374. But under certain circumstances, a limited partner can become personally liable as if he/she were a partner of a trading partnership. Thus, if a limited partnership enters into an agreement (contract) with a third party and this party when entering into the agreement neither knew nor should have known that one of the partners had entered the partnership on condition that he/she would not be personally liable, then that partner will be liable according to that agreement

(Partnerships Act, Chapter 3, section 9) in the same way as if he/she was a general partner.

A limited partner will also be personally liable, even if the third party should have known of his/her limited liability, when the partner has knowingly and purposely accepted the use of a business name not including the word *kommanditbolag* for the partnership (Partnerships Act, Chapter 3, section 9).

A third party will very rarely be able to invoke this last rule.

§3. Contributions and Division of Profits

375. The above started (see paragraph 322–326 *supra*) is applicable on limited partnerships too. However, one additional point is necessary. The Partnerships Act states, in Chapter 3, section 5, that it is for the court to decide according to equity how the profits and losses of a partnership are to be divided between the partners if the partnership agreement does not contain any provision on the division of profits and losses and the partners have not later agreed on their division. It is therefore advisable for the partnership agreement to state how the profits and losses are to be divided between the general and limited partners.

§4. The Management of a Limited Partnership

376. If the partners have not agreed otherwise, a limited partner has no right to act in the internal management of the partnership (Partnerships Act, Chapter 3, section 4). This means that a partner with limited liability has the same position as a partner in a trading partnership who does not take part in its management. He/she cannot veto actions taken by the general partner or by a limited partner who has been given the right to be involved in the internal management of the partnership. But those who may take action are not allowed without the consent of all other partners to take action that is contrary to the kind of activity for which the partnership was formed or to its purpose or that is contrary to the rule of equal treatment or the general clause (see paragraph 331 *supra*).

377. As for annual accounts and annual reports, the 1999 Accounting Act, Chapter 6, section 4, and the 1995 Annual Reports Act, Chapter 2, section 7, provide that the annual accounts and the annual report, respectively, must be signed by all partners who have unlimited liability for the obligations of the enterprise. This means that they are not signed by limited partners.

378. The rights of the partners of a trading partnership to scrutinize the accounts of the partnership and to receive information about its business, which are mandatory in a trading partnership (paragraph 328 *supra*), are rights that are also enjoyed by both general and limited partners of a limited partnership. Unlike in a trading partnership, however, the partners of a limited partnership may agree that a limited partner shall not have this right of scrutiny (Partnerships Act, Chapter 3, section 6).

379. As for the right to represent the partnership in relation to third parties, the Partnerships Act (Chapter 3, section 7) states that a limited partner has no authority to represent the partnership. This rule, which is mandatory, has the aim of protecting any third party from getting the idea that such a partner is personally liable. The Act adds, however, that the partnership will nevertheless be bound if it is represented by a limited partner and the other party neither realized nor should have realized that the person who represented the partnership was a limited partner.

The fact that a limited partner may not represent the limited partnership in his/her capacity as a partner does not preclude him/her from being given the position of a *prokurist* – see paragraph 350 *supra* – or from being provided with the authority of a proxy. In neither case may the third party be deceived into believing that he/she is liable as a general partner.

§5. Transferability of Participations

380. The Partnerships Act does not contain any special rules on the transferability of participations in limited partnerships. The provisions of the Act on trading partnerships are therefore applicable to limited partnerships. See concerning this paragraphs 352 et seq. *supra*. The partners may, for example, agree in their partnership agreement that the limited partners are to be permitted to transfer their shares in the partnership to new owners without the approval of, for example, the general partner(s).

§6. Liquidation

381. With one exception, the Partnerships Act does not include special rules on the liquidation of limited partnerships. The exception concerns one of the grounds for winding-up a partnership. The Act states that the death of a limited partner shall not be a ground for winding-up the partnership unless the partners have agreed differently (Partnerships Act, Chapter 3, section 11). But with regard to the death of a general partner, the rule is the same as for partners in trading partnerships.

As for the rest, the rules governing trading partnerships also apply to limited partnerships. This means that at this stage in the life of a limited partnership, actions concerning internal management are to be taken jointly by all the partners – both the general and the limited partners – unless they have agreed otherwise or one or more liquidators have been appointed by the court (Partnerships Act, Chapter 3, section 4).

§7. Taxation

382. Rules on the taxation of limited partnerships are largely the same as those for trading partnerships. See paragraph 369 *supra*.

Selected Bibliography

The following books can be recommended:

Andersson, Sten, Svante Johansson & Rolf Skog. *Aktiebolagslagen, en kommentar, I-III*. ISBN: 978-913901168-2.

Dotevall, Rolf. *Samarbete i bolag, om personbolag*. 3rd edn. 2015.

Fäger, Catarina & Rolf Skog. *The Swedish Companies Act*. 2007.

Giertz, Magdalena & Hemström Carl. *Handelsbolag*. 2004.

Hemström, Carl & Giertz, Magdalena. *Bolagens rättsliga ställning, Om enkla bolag, handelsbolag, kommanditbolag och aktiebolag*. 10th edn. 2013.

Hemström, Carl & Håkan Nial. *Om handelsbolag och enkla bolag*. 4th edn. 2008.

Johansson, Svante. *Nials Svensk associationsrätt*. 11th edn. 2014.

Laven, Håkan. *Arbetstagare i styrelser, kommentar till den nya lagen för privatanställda*. Publica, 1988.

Lindskog, Stefan. *Lagen om handelsbolag och enkla bolag, en kommentar*. 2nd edn. 2010.

Pettersson, Per & Annika Lundius. *Handelsbolag/Årsredovisning, en lagkommentar*. 1991.

Sandström, Torsten. *Handelsbolag och enkla bolag*. 7th edn. 2013.

Sandström, Torsten. *Svensk aktiebolagsrätt*. 5th edn. 2015.

Skog, Rolf. *Rodhes aktiebolagsrätt*. 24th edn. 2014.

Selected Bibliography

Index

The numbers here refer to paragraph numbers.

Index

www.ingramcontent.com/pod-product-compliance
Lightning Source LLC
Chambersburg PA
CBHW071346230926
51846CB00002B/466